與阿扁兄共勉：

艱困中成長的人

有最美好的理想

李遠哲 敬題

八十八年十一月

This is how I looked at the time of my graduation from primary school.

My father, Chen Sung-ken, and mother Lee Shen.

Growing up in a physician's family, Shu-chen was a multi-talented, outgoing young girl.

Self-understanding grew as a university student. I felt much better about myself after abandoning business for law.

Professor Weng Yueh-sheng let me use his study to prepare for the bar exam. Shu-chen's visits to the study were the happiest times. As a university junior I achieved the top score on the bar exam.

In 1980 I joined the Kaohsiung Incident defense team. The efforts of many of us, including David Chiang, Chang Chun-hung, Yu Ching, Frank Hsieh, Su Chen-chang, Kuo Chi-jen, and Lee Sheng-hsiung, gravitated towards political reform.

In 1984, during my stint as director, Formosa magazine published an article suggesting that Feng Hu-hsiang had passed off translation for original work in his university professor qualification thesis. Feng sued the magazine for libel, and ignoring the professional opinion of respected scholars, the Taipei District Court found Lee Yi-yang, Huang Tien-fu and me guilty. In protest, I resigned from the Taipei City Council and went to serve my one-year jail term. Upon our release after eight months, we received a tremendous popular welcome. In those days, justice only existed on the streets.

In 1985, I ran for Tainan County magistrate in protest of legal injustice. Although my campaign caused a sensation, it cost my wife lifelong paralysis from the waist down in a brutal auto attack. While I served out my jail sentence, intrepid Shu-chen courageously ran for the legislature, garnering the highest number of votes.

After becoming a legislator in 1989, I soon became known as a "sharp diamond" and was voted the top legislator by political journalists. But my proudest accomplishment was gaining the people's trust as a watchdog over military matters. Here I am pictured protesting vote buying by the ruling Kuomintang party.

My legislator's office was staffed by an energetic group of dedicated young people. When I ran for mayor in 1994, they helped form my winning campaign team.

Campaigning for Taipei City mayor, 1994.

Constantly moving on the campaign trail, I took meals and skimmed the evening paper on the fly.

Countless people lent a helping hand during my campaign. Here, one supporter helps wipe my sweat as I visit an outdoor market.

Well over 100,000 supporters gathered at our campaign headquarters to celebrate victory in the 1994 Taipei mayoral election. Joyful in victory, we solemnly swore to renew Taipei into a city of hope.

Inspecting underground rainwater drainage systems.

Inspecting progress on the Taipei Rapid Transportation Systems Chungho line.

Taking a look at the water level of the Keelung River in the wake of Typhoon Herb.

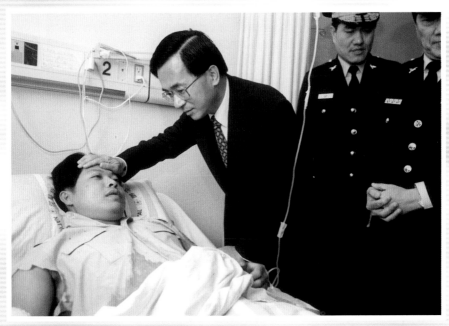

Visiting a police officer injured in a shootout with kidnapper Lin Chun-sheng.

Visiting a fish market on the eve of Chinese New Year.

As Taipei mayor, I led a delegation of medical professionals, including the Taipei City Department of Health, to the offshore island of Kinmen to show concern for the shortage of medical supplies on the front line.

With President Lee Teng-hui during his visit to the mayor's office.

Huang Hsin-chieh inspired me to transfer from business school to pre-law, and later influenced my decision to enter into politics. Up until his death in November 1999,

Pictured here with Formosa Plastics Group Chairman Wang Yung-ching, keynote speaker at an Industry and Economics Summit hosted by the Taipei city government.

Academia Sinica President Lee Yuan-tseh extended his full support to City Hall's efforts at community transformation.

Pictured here with Kim Dae-jung during a 1995 visit to Seoul. Two years later, his National Congress for New Politics (NCNP) toppled Korea's ruling party, and as president he helped Korea weather the Asian economic crisis.

The same year, I was the only representative of Taiwan invited to a roundtable conference in Japan in preparation for the upcoming APEC meeting.

From May 27-29 1998 Taipei hosted the first World Capitals Forum, attended by representatives of 67 cities from 58 countries despite an all-out campaign by Beijing to discourage attendance.

After four years in office, our city government team boasted a 76% approval rating. The billboard pictured here reads "I'm smiling, because Chen Shui-Bian has done a good job!"

During the 1998 Taipei mayoral campaign "A-Bian caps" sold like hotcakes, demonstrating the public's approval of our energetic style and hope for a better future.

Our City Hall team accomplished a great deal during our four-year term, but for the re-election campaign we outlined a 101-point program under the slogan "hope is on the move" emphasizing the work left to do.

As the votes came in, sealing my failed re-election bid for mayor of Taipei, I was comforted by thoughts of Churchill's defeat following victory in World War Two.

THE	TOP	TEN	CITIES

Europe	Asia	South America
1 LONDON, U.K.	1 SINGAPORE	1 SANTIAGO, CHILE
2 PARIS, FRANCE	2 TOKYO, JAPAN	2 MONTERREY, MEXICO
3 GLASGOW, U.K.	3 OSAKA, JAPAN	3 BUENOS AIRES, ARGENTINA
4 ZURICH, SWITZERLAND	4 HONG KONG	4 RIO DE JANEIRO, BRAZIL
5 GENEVA, SWITZERLAND	5 AUCKLAND, NEW ZEALAND	5 MEXICO CITY, MEXICO
6 AMSTERDAM, NETHERLANDS	6 SYDNEY, AUSTRALIA	6 SAO PAULO, BRAZIL
7 OSLO, NORWAY	7 MELBOURNE, AUSTRALIA	7 CIUDAD JUAREZ, MEXICO
8 NICE, FRANCE	8 SEOUL, SOUTH KOREA	8 BRASILIA, BRAZIL
9 FRANKFURT, GERMANY	9 TAIPEI, TAIWAN	9 SAN JUAN, PUERTO RICO
10 MUNICH, GERMANY	10 PUSAN, SOUTH KOREA	10 CARACAS, VENEZUELA

In 1997, Taipei made Fortune magazine's list of Asia's best cities for business. In 1998, ASIAWEEK placed Taipei fifth among Asia's most livable cities, erasing our city's reputation as an ugly duckling. At bottom right is a special report on Taipei City by Japan's Nikkei magazine.

At the end of the century, the international media devoted considerable attention to picking leaders for the next millennium. In 1994, I was picked by TIME magazine as one of the world's "young leaders for the new millennium." In 1998, Business Week magazine chose me and Academia Sinica President Lee Yuan-tseh for its list of 50 Asian leaders at the forefront of change. In 1999, ASIAWEEK listed me among its 20 leaders for the new millennium.

After stepping down as mayor of Taipei, my "learning tour" gave me a new perspective on the people's concerns.

A visit to aborigines on the offshore island of Lanyu.

Despite the tragedy of the 19 September 1999 earthquake, children's smiles show us hope for the future.

Taiwan library 1

The Son of Taiwan

The Life of Chen Shui-Bian and his
dreams for Taiwan

by Chen Shui-Bian

Translator David J. Toman

Proof reader N.Yang

Taiwan Publishing co.,Ltd.

Brother A-Bian:

People who grow up with less
Have the sweetest ideals

Lee Yuen-tseh
(President, Academia Sinica)
November 1999

Preface by Wang Yung-ching
Chairman, Formosa Plastics Group

As we all know, Chen Shui-Bian comes from a background in law. He demonstrated outstanding capability as a junior in university, when he passed the national examinations and qualified to practice law professionally. Later, he put himself on the line as a lawyer for the defense in the Kaohsiung Incident. For this he became a political prisoner, serving time in jail, and ultimately stepping out on the road of political no return.

My first meeting with Chen Shui-Bian left a deep impression on me. Arriving with his wife, Wu Shu-chen, he got out in front of our door and carried his wife to her wheelchair. Then, after exiting the elevator, he carried the wheelchair up another flight of stairs, showing extreme care, warmth and consideration throughout. Witnessing these actions, this first meeting really touched me.

Subsequently, he came to see me regularly from time to time. Even after he was elected mayor of Taipei, despite his extremely busy schedule he still managed to keep up with his visits. Although I was unable to provide any decent suggestions, with sincerity and modesty he always said he wanted to ' seek counsel from me. 'I think these attributes show that luck has little to do with Chen Shui-Bian's outstanding accomplishments.

I like to cite the "skinny goose theory" to characterize the way in which Taiwan's various accomplishments have come about. In the early post-war years, following the end of Japanese rule and the Kuomintang's retreat to Taiwan, the people's lives were filled with hardship. In the search for survival, in typical traditional Chinese fashion, with resilience and hard work they found their way through this hardship and built their own accomplishments. This "skinny goose theory" applies well to Chen Shui-Bian as well. Born into a poor family, he had to work extra hard to seize the chances to make his mark. Never allowing discouragement to disrupt his focus, in true Taiwanese fighting spirit he only gathered steam with each setback.

His conscientious performance as a legislator and assiduous, stalwart style as mayor of Taipei amply demonstrate his intense passion for political reform, stirring appreciation deep and wide among a society eager for order. Chen's tremendous popularity has been accumulated bit by bit, one step at a time.

This is why, on the night that the results revealed he lost his bid for re-election as mayor of Taipei, a great big crowd of supporters gathered at his election headquarters, reluctant to disperse and head home. Many among the crowd were outwardly upset, their tears displaying their frustration and disappointment. Resolute in the wake of this painful defeat, they called for Chen Shui-Bian to take his talents to a higher level and run for president. Certainly, this was an unusual scene in today's world.

In this autobiography, we get a good look at the reflective side of Chen Shui-Bian. In four years, during which he threw his entire being into his role as mayor, Chen achieved some outstanding results. Yet despite widespread recognition of these achievements, the voters thwarted his quest for another term with a verdict that shocked most people. In the face of such a discouraging setback, Chen Shui-Bian chose not to become depressed or bemoan his misfortune, but rather to take a good look inside himself and examine the reasons for his failure. Before long, he adjusted his approach and set off again to boldly face the next stiff wave of challenges.

At this time, in order to broaden his global horizons and gain the knowledge and insight necessary for a potential state leader, Chen emerged quickly from the subdued mood of election defeat and embarked on visits to advanced nations to learn from their experiences in national administration. These actions amply demonstrate Chen Shui-Bian's unique pragmatic and forward-looking qualities. Taiwanese society, despite having entered the ranks of modern democratic nations, is hampered by a weak legal structural foundation, as many regulations and restrictions still await amendment and strengthening.

However, in practice, lack of sufficient know-how dictates that, in addition to taking a realistic look at the deficiencies of society today and formulating appropriate measures to address them, we must also learn from the experiences and views of advanced nations. Learning from their strengths to make up for our weaknesses, we hope to echo their progress without making their mistakes, while accelerating the democratization and rule of law in Taiwan to progress toward the ideal of a modern society. Once again, these efforts attest to Chen Shui-Bian's hard work and dedication.

In this book, we also see how political activities have kept Chen

Shui-Bian extremely busy, yet have never prevented him from looking after his family and his children's education. This is why, whenever husband and wife, father and son, or mother and daughter are together, they always radiate a joyful, bright aura. In times of family difficulty and distress, this family can fall back on their support for one another to get through whatever situation or crisis faces them and continue to stride forward. Throughout the pages of this autobiography, we are strongly impressed by the capacities for mending and rejuvenation that distinguish Chinese culture.

Mencius said:"When Heaven is going to give a great responsibility to someone, it first makes his mind endure suffering. It makes his sinews and bones experience toil, and his body to suffer hunger··· In this way Heaven stimulates his mind, stabilizes his temper and develops his weak points."

Surveying Chen Shui-Bian's life in politics, despite its many twists and turns and assorted setbacks, A-Bian has only come away with greater courage each time, exhibiting a capacity for storing the incredible energy needed to propel him to the next level of achievement. As he faces more struggles to come, here's hoping that he seizes the opportunities at hand to put his gifts to work for the betterment of society and country.

Wang Yung-ching
November 1999

Author's Preface

New Century, New Hope

Starting with nothing, my life to this point has been similar to the majority of Taiwanese: from the ground up, escaping poverty, and entering life with far broader possibilities. Despite various limitations, I have tried to broaden my purpose and my energies to maximize the possibilities in life.

While expanding our own possibilities, all the inhabitants of this island of Taiwan compose a symbiotic community, sharing love, interacting with one another, and building our home together. The lessons learned and deeds made in this life will together become a part of history.

This book represents my life, thinking, and vision as relates to the first half of my life. It touches upon self-analysis, personal growth, thoughts on management, views on leadership, and concern for public issues. Throughout, it is unified by my devotion and love for Taiwan.

Before Taiwan, the land and its industrious people, I am sincerely humbled, and tremendously proud to be Taiwanese. As an immigrant society, Taiwan is our home, no matter when our ancestors or we arrived. As a new family, we must work together to build new hope for the new century.

Like others, as I've lived on and given of myself to this island, I am always full of expectation and hope for a more peaceful, wonderful Taiwan.

Anticipating the millennium as I write this, I know that in the near future we must not only surmount the Y2K bug, but more importantly come to recognize the essence of the millennium. This way, our collective efforts can be transformed into the power to propel Taiwan farther ahead, and prepare us to enter the new century as an invaluable player in the new global civilization.

Contents

Chapter One

Learning and Transformation

Life is truly like a magical journey⋯ That evening, I failed in my quest for re-election as mayor of Taipei. At that moment, I could hardly have imagined the journey of reflection and learning upon which I would soon embark, and which would ultimately set me on the presidential campaign trail. Coincidentally, the September 21, 1999 earthquake that shattered so many Taiwanese hearts also struck at night. Despite the loss of countless lives, the quake awakened the Taiwanese people's spirit; the usual indifference suddenly vanished, as everyone seemed to join the forces of volunteers. Defeat and disaster are a lot like the poverty of my youth: transcend it, and it can become the most magical gift of all in life.

A heart-wrenching night — failure to gain re-election as mayor of Taipei

On a winter evening in 1998, the night election results were counted for the 3-in-1 election (elections in Taipei and Kaohsiung, municipalities directly under the central government, for both city council and mayor, plus representatives in the Legislative Yuan) held earlier in the day, I lost my bid for re-election as mayor of Taipei.

As the television screen revealed the statistical breakdown, I knew clearly in my heart the harsh reality: I had lost. Before the final results were made official, support and reassurance poured in from all quarters. As information came in from our six district campaign offices, and the heads of the various city government departments and offices made their way one after another to our election headquarters, I knew that they were coming to accept the fact of failure together. Still, I couldn't help but think that the crowd of supporters gathered outside our campaign headquarters might not be fully prepared to accept our defeat.

It was unbelievable but true: Chen Shui-Bian, the perpetual motion machine always at work, always chasing after number one, had lost. This was not what I had anticipated, but it had ultimately become reality. That night, on the evening of my defeat, I made a resolution. This defeat was a test handed to me by the citizens of Taipei. Still, I resolved to treat it not as a failure, but as a gift, just as the poverty of my childhood had been a gift motivating me to keep pressing forward all these years.

In all my years in politics, my failure to gain re-election as mayor of Taipei, coming at the very height of my political career, was a severe setback. Nevertheless, having accepted defeat, the aspect of the outcome that most concerned me was whether I received a higher number of votes this time around compared to the first election, for growth in votes would indicate Taipei's support for our entire City Hall team. I am pleased that our number of votes did in fact grow, from just above 615,000 votes in 1994 to more than 688,00 votes in 1998. Moreover, our support grew in each of the city's 12 administrative districts.

The crowd grew ever larger. Some cried in anguish, while others were overcome with grief.

I thought back to prior to the election and what my wife, Shu-chen, had said: if we won, Taipei would be able to keep a sincere, hard-working mayor, and she would set off firecrackers for the people of Taipei; but if we were unable to gain re-election, she would still light those firecrackers, because at least she would have her own husband back. That is how she faced the election, with perfect equipoise and freedom from pressure. It was Shu-chen who exhorted me then to hurry back to campaign headquarters to express my admiration and gratitude to our supporters.

I recalled when I was a university freshman, such a long time ago. By chance, I encountered her at a meeting of students from southern Taiwan who were studying in the northern part of the island. She was so vivacious and full of energy, and although I was quite a pro when it came to studying, I was still just a bashful country youth. Nevertheless,

I set my mind on pursuing her then and there.

I also remembered when she suffered the accident that put her in a wheelchair for the rest of her life[1]. On the way to the hospital, worried that our young son and daughter might lose their mother, she asked if she was going to die. The rest of the way she was silent, not because she was frightened, but because she could feel her heart close to stopping and the life slipping away from her. She wanted to keep all her strength to go on living for her children.

For so many years, and having gone through so much, she has always supported me quietly in every way. Indeed, life is truly amazing.

It was already late by the time I arrived at campaign headquarters. Not only was the crowd still strong, but it was still getting larger as more people arrived. This was something I never could have imagined. I had lost an election once before, on November 16, 1985, failing to win a bid for Tainan County magistrate. On that evening, less than 100 people stayed around to listen to my concession speech, including campaign staff!

Why? Why was such a large crowd gathered here? I felt guilty inside. Having failed to gain re-election, I had disappointed the hopes of all those supporters out there. I was on the verge of shedding tears, having worked so hard for so long, and having let down so many

---

[1] For a more complete description of the deliberate attack on Wu Shu-chen, see Chapter Two.

people. But I couldn't allow myself to cry for fear of stirring up the crowd.

'How can I express my thanks to the people gathered here tonight? How can we ensure that this gathering ends peacefully?' These thoughts kept going through my head. Tonight I must tell myself firmly: 'As long as everything remains calm, it will be perfect.'

At the podium, looking out over the crowd, I thought about all the emotion gathered there: all the hurt, all the tears, all the frustration, and all the reluctance to accept the ultimate result of the election. Despite the commotion in my heart, appealing to reason I told myself that my obligation and responsibility was to maintain control over the situation, for tonight must be peaceful.

Politics requires a balance of emotion and reason. With emotion in store, I can draw on the passion needed to involve myself and the people in public issues. By the same token, without reason how can one make clear judgments and calm, level-headed decisions?

On the platform that night, I wanted so much to express more emotion in response to the crowd's fervor, but I couldn't do so. I was also thinking that, having lost the election, I could now go home and spend more time with my wife, which was in itself a gain despite the overall defeat. Maybe it was as my wife, Shu-chen, had said, and we could put our minds at ease and set off those firecrackers. With these thoughts I regained a clearer mind and a better perspective on everything that had happened.

"Chen Shui-bian, run for president! Chen Shui-bian, run for president!" Fervent chants rose, coming like a tide from the square. At the time, I took them as reassurance and encouragement from our supporters. I was a bit worn out and looked forward to getting some rest, recharging my batteries, and spending some quiet time. Ever since becoming involved with politics, always pushing ahead, I have had hardly any time off. Now, it would be time to gather thoughts and conduct an overall assessment.

From the rostrum I made my concession speech. I characterized my state of mind best when I spoke these words: "Severity toward a progressive team is the mark of a great city." Despite our accomplishments, validated by such a high public approval rating and an unprecedented number-five ranking (after Japan's Tokyo, Fukuoka, and Osaka; plus Singapore) among Asia's best cities by ASIAWEEK magazine, we still lost the election.

Up on the platform, Shu-chen joined the entire city government team as we bowed deeply to show our gratitude to our supporters and say, 'Sorry. We lost.'

That evening, taking in the zeal of the crowd below, how could my mind remain untouched? Yet unlike most others, who could let it all out with a good cry, I needed to hold back the emotion and maintain firm reason. I suppose that is a part of the price you pay when you become involved in politics.

That evening I told myself I need a relaxed, peaceful sleep. I reassured myself that the decision of Taipei's citizens was surely the right one, so I should be able to set my mind at ease and have a good rest.

From that time on I would spend more time with my wife and children, and maybe play with our dog, "Honey." Now that I was no longer the mayor, I could do a good job of being the head of my household!

Little did I realize it, but popular support is like the Mandate of Heaven, constantly pushing me on the road to running for president of Taiwan in the 2000 election.

Post-election reflection and learning

In my bid for re-election as mayor of Taipei, I lost to Ma Ying-jeou, representing the Kuomintang (KMT), Taiwan's ruling party. Analysis of the election results revealed that the overwhelming majority of "mainlanders"[2] in Taipei cast their votes for Mr. Ma.

---

[2] The term *Waishengren* originally described the approximately 1.5 million people who followed the Nationalist Kuomintang (KMT) government in its retreat to Taiwan from China between 1947 and 1949, following its defeat in the Chinese civil war at the hands of Mao Zedong's communists. Today, the term is still applied to those uprooted survivors and their descendants, now reaching well into the second and third generations. Always a quantitative minority never accounting for more than 15% of Taiwan's population, with the dismantling of the martial law structure and the progressive democratization of Taiwan, the *Waishengren* have become disenfranchised as "native Taiwanese" (those whose families had settled in Taiwan prior to 1949) have reclaimed key positions in government and society, leading to a collective sense of distrust and anxiety that bonds these "mainlanders" together despite decades of intermarriage and assimilation into Taiwanese society.

Regardless of how various pundits and media in Taiwan and abroad assess the election results, I accept personal responsibility for the defeat. Responsibility for the outcome rested fully upon my shoulders — no excuses. During the campaign, I saw the firecrackers, signs of celebration and good fortune, set off by all my supporters. But what I failed to see was that, in many places I did not reach and did not detect, so many people had already made up their minds to cast their vote for Ma Ying-jeou.

Despite the consistently high approval rating, despite citizens' considerable appreciation of the city government corps, we still lost. I needed to pause and reflect on this.

Following the election defeat, I listened hard to advice from all quarters, settled back down, and did some reading and thinking. I realized that I could in no way use the unique make-up of the Taipei City electorate as an excuse for my failure to stay in City Hall. I knew I must take stock of my words and actions, and my style of communication to figure out why the "mainlander" population lacks trust in me, and I must treat this as an opportunity to reflect on my approach. I hoped that on the upcoming "night of appreciation," members of the mainlander population might be able to tell me frankly where I had come up short or not done enough.

I learned that the suspicion and mistrust by the mainlander population was rooted in the gaps in background and identity separating us. We did not share enough common ground on such issues as ideology, as well as the future status of Taiwan (*de jure* independence vs. eventual unification with China), so despite their high approval rating of my overall performance they still voted for my opponent, Ma Ying-jeou. I knew that I would have to devote effort to bridging these differences in the future.

This election was also an awakening for me, a person who has always been quite self-assured, in that it reinforced the fact that confidence is necessary, but over-confidence can be a bad thing. One needs to keep an open mind to leave room to accommodate diverse opinions and standpoints.

I also devoted considerable thought to criticism of my "domineering" or overly aggressive image. I have always tried to exemplify tenacity and diligence, two qualities I consider vital. Nevertheless, both tenacity and diligence can be communicated in softer, non-abrasive ways with patience and warmth. When I first took office as mayor of Taipei, I saw so many areas in which the city needed to improve. Knowing that I only had four years to alleviate so many accumulated ills made me appear heavy handed in several areas of policy, as I gave little thought to how focusing directly on eliminating these ills would affect people. In light of criticism along these lines, I admonished myself, saying that while I could be firm about objectives in the future, I must take a softer approach. That said, in the event of a situation where determination and a soft approach cannot be reconciled, such as in the battle against crime, corruption, or the sex industry, I will stick to my guns and take the inevitable criticism, for I have a zero-tolerance policy against such conduct and no room for gray areas.

Although it still appears as if *waishengren* ("mainlanders") remain wary of me, during my term as mayor of Taipei I am confident that so-called "ethnic differences" in personnel matters or in administration of policy never colored my handling of personnel matters or administration of affairs. Ethnic differences, known literally as "provincial identity"[3] , is a sensitive and serious issue at the core of anxiety not just for citizens of Taipei, but for everyone in Taiwan. Exhaustive and close communication is imperative for forging common ground on these issues.

Over the years, whenever discussion turned to Taiwan's future or the future development of cross-strait relations, *waishengren* have generally become uneasy and distrustful toward the Democratic Progressive Party (DPP), including myself. We can credit the long-term monopoly of the media by the KMT for perpetuating these myths.

Similarly, with each election the KMT plays its "stability card" to its own benefit, thereby solidifying a regime maintained partially upon unholy alliances with money and organized crime.

---

[3] The term *Waishengren*, used to refer to arrivals from the Chinese mainland with the Kuomintang (Nationalist) government, literally means "people from outside the province." Thus, despite general consensus in Taiwan that the island is a separate and equal "political entity" from the People's Republic of China, the terminology of the past — when Taiwan was considered a province of China — has carried over into the present. *Benshengren* (lit. "people from this province"), the term commonly used to describe "Taiwanese" — usually defined as those who came to Taiwan themselves or whose descendants were settled in Taiwan before the arrival of the Kuomintang — also centers upon the word *sheng*, or "province." Given the outdated thinking and unnecessary division implied by such terms, it is no wonder that politicians and scholars alike have settled on the somewhat empty yet nevertheless attractive inclusive term "new Taiwanese" in the attempt to bridge divisions and foster greater cohesiveness within society.

Taiwan and China are two separate governments, neither subject to the jurisdiction of the other, which exercise their own respective sovereignty. About this there is no question. However, a unique historical background and legacy have allowed the Kuomintang to remain in power, where it has indulged the one-two punch of money and mob interests —known locally as "black-gold" politics[4] —to maintain its grasp on power. Indeed, a seemingly endless list of examples, including public works bid rigging, a murder committed in full view of others by a county assembly speaker, and the destruction of national land and public security, makes one wonder if Taiwan has indeed achieved "independence" —as the "Republic of Money and the Mob!"

It is incredible to consider that the CKS International Airport phase two expansion project, originally priced at somewhere between ten and twenty billion new Taiwan dollars (NT$10 billion is roughly equivalent to slightiy over US$30 million), was nearly inflated to several tens of billions of NT dollars when organized crime conspired to drive the cost up. Had their scheme succeeded, this project alone would have lined the pockets of mobsters with untold sums of taxpayers' money.

---

[4] Black-gold politics: "Black" represents organized crime, while "gold" denotes big money interests. Taiwan's ruling party, the KMT, has skillfully exploited relations with big business and triads (organized crime) to mutual advantage for decades. During the martial law period, when the KMT ruled Taiwan with an iron fist, big business and the underworld answered to the government. However, in the decade of liberalization since the lifting of martial law, the KMT is widely viewed as having swapped roles, answering to its former minions in exchange for their contribution of support and muscle to maintain its hold on power.

Black-gold politics must come to an end, but only when there is no permanent ruling party and the former opposition party can take power can this end come about. Nevertheless, Taiwan's populace seems to accept this fact on an intellectual level, but on a behavioral level they remain reluctant to support the Democratic Progressive Party (DPP). The DPP must pause to reflect on this, and deal with their distrust.

In the year since losing the mayoral election, from investigating the causes of my election failure, to national security, to cross-straits relations, I have learned from scholars and experts, listened to public opinion, and devoted my own efforts to reading classic works and settling down to reflect. Throughout this process I have gained like never before, and I consider this an unexpected side benefit of failing to regain the mayor's seat.

This is also why I subsequently proposed the "New Middle Road Hinging on National Security" political platform. I believe that the people of Taiwan must enter into a public contract of trust with one another, and that only on the basis of this trust can we both seek progress and resist outside pressure.

In my free time, I occupied myself with deep reflection and learning from exchanges with scholars and experts on a multitude of issues. I knew that I must enhance my learning and sensibilities before going on to seek progress. Like countless other Taiwanese, seeking betterment, motivated by inexorable will and relying on tough resilience to escape the poverty of the past and create today's wealth, hadn't I taken the same path? Now, it was time for me to absorb more from the Taiwanese spirit!

Following the election, calls for me to run in the 2000 presidential election rose from all corners of society. At first, I gave little thought to these pressures. On the one hand, more than anything, I needed to get away and learn new things, while on the other I longed to spend more time with my family, living my own life. After all, as a political figure occupied each day with public matters, opportunities to learn, recharge, and be with family are rare.

I wanted to know Taiwan better, understand what the public was thinking, and look into the possibilities for Taiwan's future.

Opening my heart and mind to listen to the breathing and heart beat of Taiwan, I began my "learning tour," "tour of the land," and "industry tour."

From countryside to city, from fields to science parks, I sought guidance from all corners of society to help foster a fuller appreciation of Taiwan today. From agriculture to high-tech, from anonymous locals to prominent successful figures, I sensed the vitality present in Taiwan. In the Taiwanese, I saw the finest qualities of humanity.

In addition, I received lessons from leaders of the religious community, who taught me about compassion and wisdom. Through this, I began to understand that the Chen Shui-Bian of the past indeed had a number of faults and failings.

By September 1999, I had visited all 309 administrative localities in Taiwan, from the smallest hamlet to the largest city. Having completed this marathon of sorts, I was invigorated with an ineffable strength from inside.

In Changhua County's Fenyuan village, I came across some old pineapple growers. The harvest was unexpectedly good this year, but the agricultural cooperative was unable to purchase their surplus. Setting the price extremely low, they put up roadside tents and sold the pineapples themselves. Even though the price was a pittance, they couldn't allow the unsold pineapples to spoil and go to waste. In other words, they couldn't allow the fruits of the land to be thrown away. Their work was taxing and difficult, yet they acted so responsibly and worked so hard. How I hoped to have the opportunity to thank them on behalf of the land and work to help them secure better safeguards and compensation.

In science parks, I saw technicians in high-tech industries producing information electronics products. Whether in terms of quality, production output, or worldwide market share, their work is impressive, for they are forging a new "Taiwanese miracle."

Coming from a poor environment, I have already been amply blessed with opportunities to serve as an elected representative and as mayor. I have worked tirelessly, seeking achievement, growing and struggling just like every other Taiwanese person —progressing from nothing to something, acting purposefully at every step.

"And so Taiwan will become a fine place, 300 years hence she will be known to everyone," so says an old folk song. Today, Taiwan is already a fine place; in fact the island is "swimming in money" if a local saying holds true. However, a secure, righteous, and equitable Taiwan has not yet arrived. I am prepared to work toward this kind of Taiwan with my compatriots. Before the land of Taiwan, I feel both very lucky and very humble.

Like everyone else, I am responsible for Taiwan. Taiwan is a gift to us from Heaven, and we should respond by making ourselves gifts to Taiwan in kind. Everything we do today should be considered a gift to Taiwan. Sure enough, "Taiwan is a fine place," but we must work together toward the objective of a secure, righteous, equitable Taiwan.

Thanks to a momentary defeat, I was able to move around, therefore seeing more and learning more. I see the island of Taiwan, but I know that there is more to Taiwan than what I see; the "fine place" of which we dream is more than this. I envision a future, and that future must begin today.

Communication tours: From city diplomacy to strategic security

In 1999, I embarked upon a series of trips, together comprising an "Asia-Pacific Security Communication Tour." This tour took me to Japan, South Korea and Mongolia, where I met with government officials, members of key think tanks and decision-makers, to exchange ideas and enhance mutual understanding.

I also conducted a "Strategic Security Tour" to the United States, to get to know Washington, D.C., and familiarize myself with the thoughts and perceptions of American officials and citizens. In addition, I expressed to them in no uncertain terms that Taiwan's security, dignity, and development must be safeguarded and supported. After all, **a free and democratic Taiwan is a crucial component of global strategic security, as well as a part of American interests.**

International liaisons such as these did not just begin recently. In fact, during my term as mayor of Taipei I worked tirelessly promoting "city diplomacy" in hopes of taking both Taipei and Taiwan out to the world and keep from disappearing from the global stage.

Under pressure and isolation from China, diplomacy is extraordinarily difficult for Taiwan. Nevertheless, people facing adversity do not have the luxury of despair; we must think smarter and work harder.

I remember the first time I went abroad for a political visit. A Taipei City councilman at the time, I took part in a city diplomacy trip led by council speaker C.P. Chang. Back then, travel abroad was difficult due to domestic restrictions, so many council members wanted more than anything to travel abroad at public expense during their term. Frequently, in order to visit a sister city, they could arrange to visit a number of countries and places unrelated to the stated mission of the tour. Little real thought or effort went into promoting city diplomacy, and the tours practically amounted to disguised global tourism.

When I was a legislator, both the ruling party and the opposition often formed groups to travel abroad, but during meals KMT members would sit together at one table, and DPP members at another. Our inability to unite and work together without barriers between us certainly astonished our international friends as they wondered whether we were really from the same country.

My experience on overseas trips as a city councilman and legislator told me that unwillingness to make efforts and factionalism prevented concentration of forces and focus of collective energy. City councilors represent Taipei, and legislators represent the whole country. There is only one Taiwan, only one country, and by the same token the collective objectives of diplomatic interests and national development are singular. Party divisions cannot be allowed to cleave overall diplomatic efforts.

Having gained election as mayor of Taipei as the Democratic Progressive Party's nominee, I was proud to be a member of the DPP. Yet following my election I was no longer just the DPP's mayor. but Taipei's mayor regardless of party affiliation or ethnicity. Consequently, when I took the oath of office before the flag, or when I participated in the new year's flag-raising ceremony, I did so in the capacity of the mayor of Taipei, Republic of China. Paying my respects to the flag indicated acknowledgement of the facts, and acceptance of the mainstream consciousness of the people. When I went on visits abroad or conducted city diplomacy, I had diplomatic and national interests and the interests of the Taiwanese people in mind.

Thanks to numerous visits abroad, I know that many things that everyone believes impossible can actually be accomplished; it just depends on how smart you are, how much you think, and how hard you try.

In 1996, breaking precedent, Taipei was able to participate in the first Cities of Asia Pacific Conference, held in Brisbane, Australia. At first, since Brisbane has a sister city relationship with China's Shenzhen, and given Taiwan's lack of official diplomatic relations with Australia, the organizers only invited Beijing, Shanghai, Shenzhen, and Guangzhou and did not extend an invitation to any Taiwanese city. Nevertheless, by working various channels we were able to achieve a breakthrough when the organizers sent a belated invitation to Taipei, as well as Taichung and Kaohsiung. In response, China warned the organizers that if representatives from Taiwan attended they would withdraw from the proceedings. Sure enough, when we attended the conference, China withdrew as threatened. During the conference, attended by the mayors and representatives of over 30 cities hailing from over 20 countries, each country's flag flew outside the conference hall, including the flag of the Republic of China. There, the Pacific Rim's major cities felt our perseverance and presence.

Throughout my term as mayor, I spent considerable effort on city diplomacy, so that Taipei City and all of Taiwan could go out and meet the rest of the world. Never giving up on any possibility, we worked hard at setting a stage for Taiwan. Our city diplomacy not only worked in line with the plans of the Ministry of Foreign Affairs, but was also proactive, seeking points of penetration, accumulation of energy, and qualitative improvement. For instance, Ulan-Ude, capital of Russian Federation member-state the Republic of Buryatia, the Mongolian capital of Ulan Bator, and the Polish capital of Warsaw, all established sister city relations with Taipei and have continued to maintain active contacts with Taipei.

Of all our accomplishments in city diplomacy, I was most heartened by our active participation in the U.S.-Japan Guidelines for Defense Cooperation (IULA). I personally attended the Union's 1995 and 1997 world conferences in the capacity of world body executive committee member and member of the Asia-Pacific chapter. The 1997 world conference in Mauritius was chaired by the mayor of Santiago, Chile. He proposed that in addition to a biannual world conference, a World Capitals Forum (WCF) should also be held.

At this proposal, I suggested that a meeting of the WCF every two years was too long between meetings, and that I hoped the mayors of the world's capitals could get together and exchange experiences and thoughts on urban issues once each year. I also expressed the hope that the first such annual meeting could be held in Taipei.

Building upon extensive contact with various city mayors and the growing friendships among us, the first World Capitals Forum (WCF) was held in Taipei in May 1998. Naturally, China did all it could to impede the proceedings, yet the participation of 67 cities from 58 different countries won Taiwan recognition, distinction, and friendship. The conference's success can ultimately be attributed to the cooperative efforts of the Taipei municipal government, the Office of the President, the Ministry of Foreign Affairs, the Taipei City Council, and various private sector agencies.

When it comes to diplomacy, there is no room for distinctions between government and civilians, or for egotism; rather, successful diplomacy requires hard work and cooperation. Given Taiwan's status in the global arena, we face enormous difficulty forging our own diplomatic path. Nonetheless, as long as we have the purpose, the thinking, and the objectives necessary, we can make the most of our resources and step out bit by bit. Reaching the goals in our minds requires diverse involvement, mutually beneficial interaction and exchange on an international level, and participation in international organizations and events as a means to take us closer to our objectives.

In 1999, I traveled to Japan to call on political leaders and top think tanks. My trip happened to coincide with the cherry blossom (*sakura*) season. The blossoms blanketed the landscape like a vast sea, simply breathtaking in their beauty.

Beyond the *sakura* fields I paused to think. It struck me that nothing symbolizes the "beauty of the group" more than this scene, row after row of cherry blossoms unfolding on the hillside. For me, the *sakura* provided inspiration as well as beauty.

With Taiwan put on diplomatic ice by the international community, the will of the Taiwanese people should be like the *sakura*, able to break through the cold winter to radiate in its beauty regardless of ethnic background, party affiliation, official, or civilian status.

On the vast grasslands of Mongolia, I saw a nation's unique landscape and vitality. Having made great progress, Mongolia is ready to rejoin the world community.

As night fell, I thought of the grassland herder's song: "The sky so vast, the land so endless, the breeze bends the grass to reveal oxen and sheep." The song portrays Mongolia the way it really is. The sky is so broad, so vast, just like our hearts ought to be. Which of the myriad beings nourished by the earth are free from difficulty and challenge?

Normally when I'm abroad I stay very busy. If I'm not attending meetings, talking with groups, or making arrangements, I'm listening to the priceless experiences of others or sharing with others my views on Taiwan. Yet when night falls and everything is quiet, a voice and a force arise within my heart.

The world is so vast, but Taiwan is my home.

One night during an overseas visit I dreamed that I was back in my hometown of Tainan. In the dream, it appeared as though I were a child again. I walked over to the home of my great uncle, who worked at Taiwan Sugar. There, I ate several bowls full of white rice.

When I awoke, I couldn't help laughing, while also feeling a bit sentimental. Back when I was growing up, Taiwan was poor, but the entire society was quite safe, and it was all so satisfying just to be able to eat white rice. Now Taiwan has become wealthy and white rice is nothing unusual at all, but society has taken away our sense of security. With black-gold politics and corruption rampant, unless we seek change Taiwan could become an island ruled by organized crime.

Times have changed and Taiwan has managed to throw off poverty, but today she faces still further, newer, and tougher challenges.

I am prepared to dedicate all my efforts in this life to fighting for a safer, more prosperous, equitable, and just Taiwan.

After the quake: hope for a "volunteer Taiwan"

At 1:47 AM on the morning of September 21, 1999, a massive earthquake centered in the area of Chichi shook the entire island of Taiwan, sending a tumultuous disaster our way just as we prepared to stride into the next millennium. The injuries, fatalities, and disappearances of compatriots shocked and saddened the whole country. Just as the earthquake turned Taiwan upside-down, it turned our hearts inside-out and tore them apart.

As a young boy, I watched my father till the fields with an iron plough, turning up openings for crops to take root and grow into the rice, fruits and vegetables that nourished us. The earth's image is often porfrayed as similar to that of a kind and loving mother who nurtures and sustains us. However, with this earthquake I finally learned the meaning of the Chinese saying, "When Heaven and earth are unjust, all beings seem as dispensable as straw dogs." In other words, we are all at the mercy of nature.

Indeed, the energy in the universe must balance out, which is why humans living under the mighty heavens have held its power in awe since the dawn of civilization. With the accumulation of knowledge and technological advancements, humans are able to understand certain patterns or laws of universal operation. We seek to apply this know-how to improve our odds and create a safer, better living space, yet our powers are limited and technology is not all-powerful. At least if we cannot prevent hardship or disaster, we can sustain the capacity for regeneration. **The one quality that sets the human race apart is the power of the will, which allows us to accept responsibility, take action, and plant flowers amidst rubble.**

Human power alone is surely outmatched by nature's force. This is why human beings live together in communities, divide labor into organizations, work and produce together, and help one another to confront various circumstances — including adversity.

I spent a long period following the earthquake in the areas struck hardest by the disaster. There, listening to people tell of their heartache and troubles, I was struck by the way some people, facing the death of a family member, become so grief-stricken that their eyes become dull and lifeless. Meanwhile, others lose everything they own in an instant. For days, during the hiatus from campaigning, I quietly wondered what could I do for others.

Other than donating money, showing concern, and listening, how could I, as a concerned citizen with no administrative resources at hand, get involved? What kind of response would do the most good?

With the first phase of post-earthquake relief efforts behind us, I flew to Japan. This was the second time I had visited the Osaka-Kobe region to observe how the Japanese protect against and respond to earthquakes. I also called on volunteer groups while there in the hopes that by sharing with them what was on my mind we could all work together to rebuild our home. Rather, in spite of inevitable earthquakes and natural disasters, Taiwan will be unaffected by them.

Whenever I had some time I would constantly stop to ponder how, in the wake of such a calamitous event, communities would best go about rebuilding, and how people would help one another, to forge a robust, dependable society.

Following the September 21 earthquake, Taiwan's religious groups and volunteer organizations beat the government to the scene, providing disaster victims with material and spiritual relief. With goodwill in their hearts, they were prepared to work hard without complaint. Self-motivated and splendidly efficient, they came to the assistance of their fellow human beings, giving a fresh glory and meaning to life.

I also saw forces of organized women, such as the "Moms and Grannies Work Brigade" set up in Nantou, attentively and pleasantly contributing to restoration work.

I thought of my experiences as mayor of Taipei, recalling that whether in the promotion of equality between the sexes or in policy governing support for the disadvantaged, a public servant can invoke official authority to really make a difference, helping various tasks develop in a more equitable, fair direction.

A political figure with good motives, a vision, and objectives can truly accomplish a great deal to make society better, thereby strengthening hope. Yet following the earthquake, we saw that in the face of a major disaster, the government in its present configuration was sluggish in its response. The deficiencies of the current structure became painfully clear when 20 hours had passed before the government could convene an emergency meeting.

Therefore, until the current system undergoes significant renovation, society must look for the government and private sector to complement each other to ensure the most basic freedom from fear. This is why I know that under the current structure, developing Taiwan into a volunteer society is a crucial route to survival. **Manifestation of a "Volunteer Taiwan" can ensure the rapid rebuilding of society, so that Taiwan can stand back up in no time at all.**

Paragons of the human spirit and great deeds, such as Dr. Albert Schweitzer and Mother Theresa, are able to give us strength in our darkest hours. Their selfless good deeds are like the brightest diamonds of the soul of humanity.

In Taiwan, many religious leaders and volunteer groups employ various spiritual appeals to awaken the goodness in the hearts of the Taiwanese people, in turn putting this goodness into action to help others. Their actions combine together into an unmistakable force in society.

As someone concerned about Taiwan, and in my capacity as convener of the Democratic Progressive Party's 921 Disaster Area Restoration Coordination Committee, I wish to promote progress toward the creation of a "volunteer Taiwan," where everyone can join together to forge a more rewarding, better society for ourselves.

So far our efforts have come to fruition in the establishment of "Volunteer Taiwan Work Stations" to assist residents in disaster areas and provide counseling and information. In addition, we have promoted adoption of children orphaned in the earthquake. As we have worked on these efforts, one vision and conviction has occupied my mind: that of a "volunteer Taiwan."

If more people join the ranks of volunteers, numerous social aid tasks can be promoted without the lost efficiency and wasted resources that come with government direction. This way, we can all accomplish more, and in achieving more we can feel better about overcoming difficulty and taking charge ourselves. After all, we are a part of others, so that when others are unable to walk, we become their legs, supporting them so they can keep on going. If someday one of us should encounter an awful unexpected circumstance, requiring the assistance of others, people would be there for us. Why ? Because we are a whole, together through better and worse.

In addition, the vision of a "volunteer Taiwan" includes noble spiritual pursuits, to allow one to become a beacon of light. In this world, where people thirst so for fame and fortune, spiritual enrichment brightens our lives and gives life different meaning.

In the aftermath of the earthquake, it is time for Taiwan to rebuild the community. "Volunteer Taiwan" is really another side of emphasis on the community, for the objectives of volunteerism are not limited to assistance and relief efforts, but also include group discussion and sharing of experiences and resources to attain focus on common vision; that is, to establish a new environment and substance for one's own community, for a self-sufficient, autonomous, friendlier, more livable community. That is why the ultimate objective of "volunteer Taiwan" is on a spiritual level, to forge Taiwan into a veritable "pure land" in which everyone wants to live.

In the disaster areas, we witnessed the most heart-wrenching human tragedies, yet at the same time we saw compatriots dedicated to relief efforts, demonstrating their goodwill through their actions. They are like bodhisattvas[5] in the mundane world, committed to rescuing others wherever they are needed.

I promised myself that over the course of the rest of my life, no matter what work I do, I shall always take part in the "volunteer Taiwan" movement. Taiwan is our home, and when it comes down to it we really all live under the same roof.

In the new Taiwanese family, no matter when you or your ancestors arrived here, nothing can knock us out of commission —not even calamities of nature —because we have more love, confidence, and hope.

Governments can learn from

---

[5] In Mahayana Buddhism, *bodhisattvas* are enlightened beings that agree to return to the mundane world to help others reach the paradise of the "Pure Land."

religious groups

I often think of Matsu, a figure in Taiwanese folk religions, who it is said guided the first Chinese settlers of Taiwan through the brutal seas at night and came to their rescue. With a benevolent heart, Matsu is like a mother.

The two gods who accompany Matsu, one with eyes that can see 1000 li[6] and the other with ears that can hear far over the horizon, represent empathy, observation, and feeling. Government should be like Matsu, equipped with acute powers of observation; see clearly to the bottom of issues, and know how to respond.

There is a hierarchy among Matsu and her attendant gods, but they divide labor according to their strengths and work together in a truly perfect "partnership."

For years, our local administrations and central authorities have been unable to establish sound partnerships. The central government concentrates power and money, which it in turn uses to engage in a top-to-bottom management approach. It uses a carrot-and-stick approach in the allocation of resources, keeping local government finances drained to the point that they are forced to implement policy more in line with the central government's needs than their own. In other words, the allocation of power between the central government and local authorities is unclear and lopsided, as the central government takes a

---

[6] The *li* is a traditional Chinese unit of measurement, approximately 1/3 of a mile or 1/5 a kilometer.

parental attitude toward controlling local governments, causing numerous problems.

For a long, long time now, the government has failed to see itself as a faithful servant of the people; it has failed to put the best interests of the people first and foremost as the reason for its own existence, so that policy constantly shifts back and forth, wasting valuable resources. During the period of the White Terror in Taiwan, the government viewed the people as evil monsters, and while that era is now behind us, today in their interaction with government people often encounter hassles and delays. As a result, they do not trust the government, and cannot view the government as their partner.

I believe that, beyond a certain point, a society's development or a country's overall progress, in addition to requiring mutual trust among citizens, requires mutual trust between the government and the people. **Only when trust is established can various forces combine together into positive partnerships —to foster mutual growth and advancement toward common objectives.**

The essence of a "volunteer Taiwan" is mutual trust, and the exponential effect of working together. Taiwanese society has already begun to progress toward this greater civilization, and as it continues to move forward, Taiwan's private sector will undoubtedly act as a solid network, acting as a security system enabling the Taiwanese people to go about their lives happily, freely, and creatively, free from fear and constraints.

Taiwan is a young society, yet having inherited certain historical burdens the government is strapped with redundant structures, making it an inefficient albatross. This is not to say the caliber of our civil servants is lacking; on the contrary, we are fortunate to have a well-educated, high-caliber civil servant corps. Inefficiency is the result of the ruling party's reluctance, blinded by its own interests, to re-organize the governmental structure. Despite its venerable history, Great Britain's Prime Minister, Tony Blair, was able to put his finger on the pulse of the times and propose a vision and administrative plan for a "young England." If England, with its long history, can revitalize itself, why can't young Taiwan? For the sake of long-term development, why can't Taiwan assess the current situation and seek new opportunities?

To the younger generation, "government" is an organization vested with public authority. They feel that its reason for existence is not to rule over the people, but rather to serve them. **The sole purpose of government is to serve the people.**

Government differs from religion in that it must weigh among various choices to satisfy assorted interests. That the give and take involved in administration must take into account the interests of the majority goes without question. Therefore, apart from harboring good will, as a religion should, government must uphold majority interests.

Government is not a volunteer group. As volunteer groups contribute to society beyond their own lives, it is not fair for us to measure how much they accomplish. In contrast, government is empowered by the people, and as such it should be an extension of the people's desires and dreams, and not become a monster alienated from its own people. Government is not a volunteer organization, but like a volunteer group, it should constantly ask itself, ' Am I upholding fairly various interests, and satisfying the mandate of the majority?'

Government should be like a convenience store, open 24 hours a day. Government should be like the Guanyin Bodhisattva, like Matsu, ready to come to the aid of others when called, and always right around the corner. In my mind, such a government is the ideal government.

I envision a certain kind of Taiwan: one where the people trust one another, and where the government is worthy of the people's trust. When mutual trust becomes a habit, it can help propel Taiwanese society into a new realm of civilization.

With this in mind, the people of Taiwan should seek a partnership based on trust, and the equitable distribution of power and resources so that in their daily lives each person feels safe, honorable, and willing to contribute their all to the common good knowing that others consider the common good as well.

History tells us that the Taiwanese people possess remarkable durability and vitality, yet the existing government structure must be thoroughly transformed. In many ways, it is like a corporation, blessed with shareholders and employees possessing unlimited potential, longing each day for innovation and reform. However, stifled by the musty, anemic policies of the top management, the company is unable to move with the times, instead basking in its past glories.

A nation is like a massive corporation —it needs sound

management and strict attention to the books. We cannot allow money interests and organized crime to collude with our management, and clean us out of our assets.

"Young Taiwan, vibrant government" is my aspiration and vision for Taiwan and our government. We should all become "shareholders" in Taiwan, to have a hand in its management. We deserve the chance to hire new top decision-makers, to engender a cleaner and more dependable government.

As "shareholders" in Taiwan, the people have the right to participate in decision-making mechanisms. Taiwan deserves better opportunities and greater room for development. To achieve these aims, we must put an end to black-gold politics, and turn a new historical page where there is no longer one permanent ruling party, but power can alternate among different political parties.

Following my failure to gain re-election as mayor of Taipei, in reassessing the relationship between the people and the government, my faith in the value of alternating political power only grew stronger. Under my direction, the Taipei City government made great improvements, nearly eliminating collusion between organized crime and money interests and putting the philosophy of service into practice. Yet despite these achievements, the people of Taipei, seeking innovation and reform, chose the Kuomintang's Ma Ying-jeou, reminding me once again that "Severity toward a progressive team is the mark of a great city." Having handed power over to a different political party, Taipei City can maintain the enhanced administrative efficiency we achieved, while a new team embarks on the pursuit of innovation. In all fairness, isn't this the ideal we seek? Having been through a period of quiet reflection, I am firmly convinced that taking the Taipei experience —including the alternation of power between different political parties —to every corner of Taiwan, will allow us to maximize our unique dynamism, releasing our youthful vitality and enabling rapid government regeneration. With an energetic, vigorous government, young Taiwan will not suffer disadvantages in meeting the challenges of the next millennium. As it turns out, not gaining re-election was in a sense a blessing in disguise, as it has given me more time to devote to Taiwan.

Chapter Two

Living and Growing

I'll always remember the wall on our home when I was growing up. The wall was always covered with a list, written in chalk, of debts and interest owed to others, including the money my father owed for my tuition. We were poor, but we never allowed ourselves to take handouts, and never passed up any opportunity for knowledge and advancement. We appreciated that material limitations must never be internalized into self-deprecation. Acutely aware that indulgence of evil brings suffering on the majority of people, after going into politics, I tried to see things from other people's point of view, and determined to never again tolerate injustice and inequity in society.

Poverty is a rare gift

The earliest partners in each of our lives are family members. Family, followed by friends, classmates, colleagues, as well as groups in society and the overall environment, affect each person's growth.

I was born on February 18, 1951 in a plain tiled house in the village of Hsichuang, Kuantien Township, Tainan County. My father was Chen Sung-ken, and my mother was Lee Shen.

My father only had a primary school education, but back in his days one had to work at the same time as studying, so he was probably only able to attend school to less than the third grade. Similarly, my mother finished third grade before leaving school to work, since my grandfather felt that girls need not have much education. Such was the reality and the limitations of that entire era. Not having the chance for a proper education, my parents had no opportunities to change their lot in life, to move up in society and escape poverty.

Despite having only graduated from primary school, my father wrote Chinese characters well and could handle arithmetic. Consequently, no matter what kind of work he took on —be it temporary work, cutting rice shoots, or bundling sugar cane —he would always handle the money when it was time to pay the workers.

My father had a good heart. Sometimes he would ask friends together for a meal, and it mattered not how much he spent on them, even if it went beyond our family's means. This was important to him, because he felt that he should be the one to pay when he went out drinking with his buddies. Still a little boy at the time, I always felt that among his many friends a few were just "fair weather friends" who showed up only when my dad was treating.

That was my dad, a generous, chummy person. He liked to drink, and as a result sometimes got out of hand, passing out in front of the local temple. I would get upset, and my mother would become angry enough to banish him from the house. But if he stayed out just a little late, my mother would become worried and go out looking all over for him. In that day and age, my father exerted himself a great deal to put food on the table, and drinking was his only recreation.

Dad would put up with anything for his family, from hard work to verbal abuse. Always willing to take on work, as soon as he was hired he would take to the hills to spray pesticides for several days on end. Even though the pungent pesticide stung his nose and throat, he never once complained.

I suppose that toiling his entire life, working beyond fatigue, getting drunk every so often, plus not wearing a mask while spraying pesticides, combined to lead to the liver cancer that took my father's life. In that era of poverty and depravation, people lived within the confines of their lot, their fortunes rising and falling with the times.

I recall how as a little boy I watched him leave for work each day, not even resting during the Chinese new year. After he completed the odd agricultural jobs he was hired for, he would come back to work on the plot or two of land he had leased from someone else. Poor materially but not in spirit, my father was an upright person. He kept the books for his bosses, always accounting for every cent. He always handled people and business according to such guiding principles, demonstrating discipline and pride in spite of poverty.

The top tube of my father's bicycle had an additional seat, upon which I like to sit and be ridden around and about by my father. I loved to ride with my father on his bike, and got to do so up until primary school when I had grown too big.

While my parents were barely beyond minimal literacy, they left an indelible impression upon me: They were conservative, laconic, never resorted to flattery, and would never show physical displays of affection, such as hugging, as today's parents often do, but they truly cared about their children. Especially during my school years, they provided enough for me to concentrate on my studies, and tried not to let helping with household chores divert my time away from schoolwork. To them, studying meant "promise" and opportunity.

I suppose that the way my parents treated me affected me profoundly. Having grown up, I found that I am a lot like them, in that I was not very good at expressing myself. Therefore, whenever I want to express a view or opinion I shoot straight from the hip, without stopping to think how I can manicure my words to be more attractive. To this day, I have maintained this direct personality, which I suppose is another kind of "inheritance."

Compared to my peers, I did little housework, but picking rice shoots or collecting sweet potatoes was definitely mandatory work for me. Especially during the summers, the Tsengwen Creek always overflowed, sending grass shoots hurtling downstream with the rushing water. There was an especially large quantity of dead wood, which we would collect as firewood. Since the muck was soft and loose, and the dead wood was heavy, often one might suddenly get sucked waist-deep into the muck. As an adult looking back upon the things we did back in those days, I realize it was quite dangerous. But we needed firewood, and being able to help my parents filled me with gratification and pride.

I often think of the example my parents set for me. For example, when we picked sweet potatoes, my mother and I would usually wait until after someone had tilled the field and dug out the largest sweet potatoes before we would pick the small ones they didn't want. As a naive child, I used to think, 'Why don't we dig before someone has ploughed the field?' But my mother admonished me, saying that would be stealing, and that was unthinkable. So although my family was poor, having been inculcated with our parents' values, none of us children ever stole anything, since it was firmly impressed upon us that we should never take what was not ours. This is also partly why, throughout my political career, I have always held nothing back in the fight against corruption and special privilege.

An old Chinese saying says that, when injustice is rampant in society, someone who steals a hairpin will be put to death, while the greedy politicians who make a mockery of the law pilfer the nation and are still appointed lords. Taiwan has come to such a point, where a minority has filched away the entire country's wealth. If we stand idly by and just let things go on, waiting for things to sort out and get better, we're gravely mistaken. Now is the time to act. My experience in leading the charge against the government's unholy alliance of organized crime and big money only confirms this conviction.

In that era of poverty, Taiwan's women had a rough time, having to work to support family while taking care of their children. I vividly recall how my mother would take me with her into the fields, and before beginning to work, she would dig a hole and place me inside to keep me from running around and bringing harm upon myself. When it was time to return home, she would come back and get me, having worked up such a sweat that the moisture from her body seeped through her clothes and onto mine as she carried me on her back.

With four children in the family and limited income, before I began working our family could never make ends meet. Always owing money, my father kept debts and interest owed written on the wall. Chalk writing always filled the wall. Figures were wiped away, only to be replaced by new ones. Despite our poverty, my parents nonetheless borrowed money so I could go to school. In turn, I made a promise to them and to myself that I would definitely make money to pay all the debts back, and to help build a new house to replace the ramshackle one the family occupied.

Having been shielded from the world by poverty, when I received a gift of blackfish caviar upon having passed the bar exam, I inspected the gift over and over and mistook it for dried papaya seeds.

Thinking back, if it weren't for education, my life would be completely different. In that era, education equaled opportunity, especially for poor people. That is why one of society's basic equalities should be equal opportunity to receive an education. This is also why I strongly disagree with the constantly rising expense of higher education under Taiwan's educational policy, as well as the prohibitive pre-school daycare costs. Children are Taiwan's future, and the hopes of their parents and society. Therefore, cultivating children is a sweet and meaningful obligation for society, and should not be just the burden of individual families or the place for harsh competition and attrition between the rich and the poor. Particularly given today's increasing globalization, fierce competition in information processing and know-how is now the norm. Knowledge is opportunity, wealth, and the future all in one. We must educate everybody, so that everyone, regardless of economic class, can hold the keys of knowledge. This is the vision and motivation behind my proposition of an "enlightened Taiwan."

As the son of a contract farmer and a poor family, I have never blamed my parents for anything. On the contrary, they gave me the chance to receive an education, and from there I relied upon my determination and diligence to make my own way in life. That is why, for me, poverty was a kind of gift. Because my background made me realize from an early age that I must work hard, and I must rely on myself.

Isn't Taiwan's "economic miracle" the product of countless others just like me, starting with nothing and working hard to make something better? Despite the pressures and limitations imposed upon us, Taiwan has held its head up high and strode proudly ahead. Power that comes from the bottom to the top is a rugged kind of power; it is the power of vitality, of searching for opportunity, sticking to convictions, getting through difficulty, and achieving things nobody believed were possible.

I know Taiwan can succeed. Because Taiwan has countless others like me, giving everything they have to make their way up from the bottom. This is also one of the many reasons justifying our unwavering confidence in Taiwan.

Taking charge of life's turning points

In the environment under which I was raised, many of my classmates came from wealthier families than I did, yet they were placed in remedial classes. The school even contributed a vegetable garden for them to cultivate. While we were studying from morning to night, they had given up, continuing that way through graduation.

They had better opportunities than I did, so why was I in the "preparatory class," while they were in the remedial class? Not that they were idle or unmotivated, but sometimes their families had the attitude that studying is no use, and they might as well help out with the family's crops. Just because their families owned a little bit of land, they never continued on in school. Others, unable to produce the NT$20 necessary for "cram school," transferred from the preparatory class to the remedial class.

My father was barely literate and worked as a hired manual laborer, but I was very lucky, for he allowed me to receive an education. He even paid my "cram school" costs and bought me additional reference books to read. I have long believed that one's environment can affect one's entire life, and that each individual's parcel in life is different. Nevertheless, if we believe that environment and fate dictate everything in life, and that we are powerless to do anything about it, we are truly mistaken. I firmly believe that as long as we are willing to set goals, and work hard towards them, we will have plenty of opportunities for success.

At graduation from Lungtien Primary School in Tainan County, I received the County Magistrate's Award, given to the top-ranked student in the class. From there, I tested into Tainan County's junior high school, and during my junior year there represented Tainan County in the first national Chinese language essay competition, placing second. Years later, my son, Chih-chung, would claim first prize in the same competition. I told him that this confirms the Chinese saying, "the pupil surpasses his master," or in this case his own father.

In 1966, I graduated from Tsengwen Junior High School with highest honors in my class, allowing me to proceed to the school's affiliated high school. However, the next year I transferred to Tainan First High School. Following the trend of the day, at first I was placed in the natural sciences section, as opposed to the social sciences section. However, after one semester of natural sciences, in which I had little interest, I found myself having a rough time of it. At first I thought I'd be like everyone else with a choice, taking the most popular pre-med. program. But before long, faced with a decision, I chose to be myself, and transferred to the social sciences section the following semester. Sometimes when a change is necessary in life, one must have the courage to go ahead and change. That way, should success come some day, at least it follows one's conscious choice.

In 1969, I graduated with the highest ranking from the Tainan First High School. As I prepared for the next step, the unified university entrance examination, I still had no particular school or department in mind. When it came time to enter my preferences, I thought of selecting law and politics. But after considering my family's conditions, I placed a few business departments ahead of law. When the results were announced, I was accepted into my first choice, the business management department at National Taiwan University.

At the time, I was convinced that if I wanted to become an attorney or a judge after graduating from the law department, I would have to participate in the national qualification examinations, which necessitated an extra step. However, if I studied business, I would be out and working soon, able to help my family pay off its debts.

So it was that I studied for a few months in the business department, yet all the while nagged by second thoughts: did I really want to just count money all the time, spending my life helping other people manage their company? I was caught in a tug-of-war between my own desires and the economic needs of my family.

In late 1969, Taiwan's first supplementary elections for central government representatives were held. Huang Hsin-chieh[7] , then serving as a Taipei City councilman, ran for a position in the Legislative Yuan. I attended a rally by the Nansung Market under the Chengchi Bridge, at which Huang presented his platform.

Huang's platform really opened my eyes. How could someone be so bold, and so openly criticize the government, taking it completely apart with such merciless reproach? Witnessing Huang's attack, I was impressed with him from the bottom of my heart. On that very evening, I made a decision. Without consulting with my parents, I determined to pursue the path of law and government.

Thinking back, if it had not been for Huang Hsin-chieh's speech that night, my life today would be completely different, and today I could very likely be a 9-to-5 business professional.

I faced another choice at the time, that being whether to finish my first year in the business school before transferring departments. However, I happened to see a newspaper report that said that National Taiwan University's department of law would be extending the law degree program to five years. At this, I thought it would be great to become a member of the law department's first five-year degree program class, and decided to sit for the entrance examination once again.

Back then, NTU's department of law was not a typical first choice, the way it is today. A case in point was the justice section, which was the last choice anyone wanted to be assigned to within the law department. Having come to the sudden decision to suspend my

---

[7] On 30 November 1999, shortly after the publication of the Chinese edition of this book, Huang Hsin-chieh died in Taipei of congenital heart failure. On 3 January 2000, at a memorial concert held at Taipei's National Concert Hall in tribute to Huang, President Lee Teng-hui called Huang "The true representative of the Taiwanese spirit."

studies, I needed to inform my parents. Returning home, I told them that I had lost interest after commencing studies in the business department. They responded, "Maybe you're not interested, but it was your own choice!" I wanted to study in the law department and be a lawyer or a judge, but there was no way they could understand how I felt. They saw it differently, that it took so much to get into university, and tuition wasn't cheap, so wasn't I merely increasing my family's burden?

I completely understood how my parents felt, and I certainly felt guilty about everything, yet I still asked them to lend me more money so I could keep studying. I had no doubt that I would soon pass the bar examination, become an attorney, and repay all debts.

After withdrawing from school, I returned home to Tainan, where I prepared to retake the entrance examination while also testing the subjects shared in common with the civil service examination, such as Chinese, history and geography, and the Three Principles of the People. That way, having already passed these subjects, I could concentrate on testing in specific law-related topics. When the unified entrance examination results were announced on August 8, 1970, I tested into my only choice, the judicial section of National Taiwan University's Department of Law, with a score of 445 points —the highest in the matriculating class.

Having gone through so much to test back into Taiwan University's law department, I took nothing for granted, studying on the one hand, while working as a tutor to help earn living expenses. In addition, maintaining excellent grades throughout my studies, I received scholarship money, eliminating further money-related issues for the rest of my university career.

I am eternally grateful to the current president of the Judicial Yuan, Mr. Weng Yueh-sheng, my university advisor, who provided his research study to me as a study place. Professor Weng's research study, unlike the dormitories, had no "lights out" time restriction, so I could study through the early morning hours. Thanks to these hard efforts, I was able to achieve highest ranking in the civil service examinations during my third year of university, earning my stripes as an attorney. Soon thereafter, in my fourth year of university, I became a practicing attorney.

Seek excellence, do what it takes; take on the role the job calls for. This is what I expect of myself. I believe that every individual has his good points and strengths, and as long as he likes something, sets his focus on a target and moves steadily toward its realization, he will never have cause for regrets no matter where he goes. The environment sends challenges our way, and we respond in kind. We must focus our determination and never give in.

He who makes swifter, more precise choices establishes the advantage. During my scholastic career I made several weighty decisions —from selecting social sciences at Tainan First High School, to sitting for the university entrance a second time to test into National Taiwan University's law department, to taking the bar exam —each time I made a decision, and each time I accepted the attendant responsibility.

Life is full of choices. Still, **the right choice should be the most reliable for you.** This is true in the life of an individual, as well as for a country's future. To paraphrase British historian Arnold Toynbee, 'From challenge to response, look for the possibility for improvement.'

Memories of a family vacation

Wu Shu-chen and I were married in 1975. Coming from a physician's family, she was the family's shining pearl, and at first my future parents-in-law were against her seeing me. I remember how I visited her in the apartment she rented on Hochiang Street near the Chunghsing University campus. There, seeing her Dacin brand wardrobe, I asked her if it was a refrigerator. At first, she assumed I liked to joke around, not believing that I really had no idea what a refrigerator looked like. Later, I became fretful after learning that my in-laws had found out about this little incident, but my fears were salved after our marriage when they came around and began treating me like their own son. For that I have always been deeply grateful. I have always been full of remorse for my in-laws especially since my involvement in politics led to the politically-motivated "vehicular assault" that left their beloved daughter paralyzed from the waist down. Just after the Taipei City mayoral election, my father-in-law, Dr. Wu Kun-chih, passed away. His death brought to mind memories of 1985, when following my narrow loss in the election for Tainan County magistrate, my wife Shu-chen became the victim of a deliberate vehicular assault. This time, just after failing to gain re-election as mayor, I lost my father-in-law. Throughout my career in politics, my family has endured a series of setbacks and traumas. This saddens me.

Standing before my father-in-law's altar, I swore that I would love his daughter throughout all my years in this life, taking care of her and our daughter. My parents and in-laws had a profound impact on my growth and that of my wife. As we go about the education of the next generation, my wife and I often remind ourselves of the various responsibilities of parenthood.

Abandoning business for law, and subsequently leaving law in favor of politics, I was making decisions that impacted greatly upon my life. I was never certain of my personal qualities from a young age, and never knew for sure what I wanted to do with my life. Looking back on my past, I see that learning about oneself is in fact quite difficult, as life is often a process of constant new endeavors. However, there are many people who, unable to achieve their own dreams, turn around and put pressure on their children to make them come true for them. This only causes torment for their children, and in the end nobody is satisfied. I have always respected the choices my daughter and son have made regarding their education. Their lives should follow their own imaginations, and as parents we can only offer suggestions and counseling, refraining from excessive intrusion or interference in their lives.

My daughter, Hsing-yu, currently a sixth-year student in dentistry at the Yangming Medical College, has absolutely no interest in politics, despite having grown up in a political environment. During my jail term, Shu-chen had been rendered immobile by the attempt on her life, but Hsing-yu showed great maturity and grew very close to her mother during that time. Having been influenced by both her maternal grandfather's occupation as a physician and Shu-chen's incapacitation, from a very young age she wanted to be a doctor. Later, when she took the university entrance examination, in order to be near home to look after her mother, she narrowed down both institutional and departmental choices, turning down other institutions' pre-med departments in favor of the dentistry program at Yangming Medical College. At one time she considered transferring to the medical department, but later became interested in dentistry, continuing on that path to this day. I think of her as our thoughtful, lovable "family practitioner." Our son, Chih-chung, is currently in his junior year at National Taiwan University's department of law, just like his father. He grew up reading political magazines, idolizing John F. Kennedy, and yearning to become "Taiwan's Kennedy!"

During my children's school years, whenever there was a mother-daughter gathering, no matter how busy I was I would always try to put everything aside so I could attend, given my wife's difficulty getting around unassisted. I was always one of a very small minority of men among the parents in attendance.

Spending time with children as they grow is a wonderful thing, but what I did cannot be thought of as taking over a mother's responsibilities or role.

Chich-chung has a wide variety of interests, and he is quite an open-minded thinker. Still, he only received 10 points on his high school entrance examination essay, preventing him from getting into Chienkuo Senior High School (Taiwan's most prestigious boy's high school). He had to settle instead for Chengkung Senior High School. At first, unable to accept the result, he became depressed. For a full month, as long as he shut himself in his room, my wife and I would become anxious. We encouraged and comforted him, but at first he wouldn't listen. Then one day I noticed on his desk an essay he had written, entitled "I Will Rise Again." For a teenager to write "I will rise again" struck me as both cute and funny, but I knew that he had become courageous and capable of facing reality.

A legislator at the time, I told him, ' Anyone who studies hard can get into Taiwan University's law department, which is made up of students from various schools, not just Chienkuo and (its all-girl counterpart) Taipei First Girl's Senior High School. I promised him that, as long as he studied hard, I would take him on a trip abroad once he got into university, and he could arrange the itinerary as he pleased. He excitedly agreed.

Three years later he really did get into National Taiwan University's department of law! Naturally, I had to keep my commitment to my son. By then I was mayor of Taipei, and very busy, but if I didn't take him on that trip it would be akin to cheating him. So rather than going back on my word and not being able to forgive myself for the rest of my life, I decided to take him on that trip after all.

Because Chih-chung is a "Kennedy buff," he wanted to visit all the places connected to Kennedy, taking us to Washington D.C., New York, Boston, and Florida. For him, Kennedy's path is his dream for life. He was so excited, and being the devotee he is he had to buy every book or souvenir having to do with Kennedy. As his father, I was responsible for carrying our bags.

While we were on vacation, news arrived from Taipei that powerful typhoon "Winnie" had caused the injury and death of Taipei residents. This news both saddened and shocked me, and several aides suggested that I rush back to Taipei. Tormented inside, I thought that as mayor I had better return, but as a parent I should finish the trip with my son. It was so contradictory: if I left my son to my wife, who could barely take care of herself, where would she find the energy to travel with Chich-chung? After careful consideration, and having taken care of relief effort arrangements, I returned to the belief that the city government is like a company, where the vice chairman (deputy mayor) is there when the chairman (mayor) is away, and the managers at all levels can take responsibility. To me, this was the definition of a solid city government team. During the remainder of the vacation, I stayed in constant touch with Taipei via telephone and fax, getting updated on the situation, communicating and providing direction, and taking appropriate measures in response. In the end, our city government team proved it was up to any difficult task.

City council members were unforgiving, and public opinion included some criticism, yet I felt that the purpose of division of labor and assignment of position is to complete tasks, and that neither rescue or restoration tasks were held up because of my absence. My thinking at the time was that, when it came to the roles of mayor and parent, that of a parent is irreplaceable. I let my city government team take administrative responsibility, while I did what I had to do as a parent. Caught in a difficult position, I was able to strike a balance between the two roles.After returning to Taiwan, my son wrote an essay, "The Potomac River Under Reflection," in which in addition to praising the history, architecture, and civilization of the United States, he added:

"What I really revere is the New World spirit that new immigrants exude while pioneering and challenging the unknown in pursuit of their dreams!"

Kennedy once said, "I believe that the times require imagination, and courage, and perseverance. I'm asking each of you to be pioneers toward that new frontier."

In his essay, Chich-chung wrote: "Perhaps tangible frontiers have already been completely opened. Nevertheless, we still have frontiers of culture, truth, and peace, and as long as our hopes have yet to be realized, as long as our troubles have yet to be eliminated, we have no reason to give up seeking, or to cease our actions." The vacation turned out to be a journey of learning for both father and son.

Throughout the trip, I couldn't put Taipei out of my mind. Tormented on the outside and inside, yet witnessing the national strength, and the advanced civilization of the United States, I was filled with emotion. Like Chich-chung, many of Taiwan's youths are filled with ideals. For our part, we must create an environment that provides them greater opportunity, and accompany them through this vital period of growth.

Each individual must face the call of the land, seeking to forge a deeper spirit, to have will, good judgment, and the courage to act. This is the new image and new future I have in mind for all Taiwanese, and where our future lies.

Going for it! Taking the political road

From a practicing attorney, I became a political figure. Apart from the impact of my personality, this transformation was a product of circumstance.

I began practicing law during my junior year of university. Following graduation, I married and started a family, working hard to provide for my growing family, and to pay off parents' debts. Having grown up under the shadow of poverty, I could finally shake it off forever. Work demanded a considerable amount of my time and effort, but I felt contented and fortunate inside. As a lawyer specializing in maritime commerce, I didn't need to deal with criminal cases or political cases, and while work occupied a great deal of my time I was able to handle it with aplomb.

With a family and career and plenty of food on the table, I began to consider going abroad to pursue an advanced degree, or taking some time to contribute to society via public service, to give different meaning to life.

Little did I know that on 10 December 1979 the Kaohsiung Incident would transpire, and that within a short three or four days the Kuomintang would begin a massive operation to arrest those involved. Yao Chia-wen and Lin Yi-hsiung, members of the Chinese Comparative Law Society, are also fellow alumni of the Taiwan University department of law a few classes ahead of me. Our paths having crossed long before, I knew what they were about, and had seen how they expressed their positions on democratic politics. That they were accused of sedition, for which the punishment was mandatory death, aroused nothing short of fury!

One day early in 1980, attorney Chang Teh-ming, currently a member of the Control Yuan, called to tell me that the defense lawyers for the Kaohsiung Incident case had been all but settled, and that only Huang Hsin-chieh and Chen Chu[8] still needed defense attorneys. At this, he asked me if I were interested in taking on their cases.

I thought back to my freshman year of university and Huang Hsin-chieh's lecture —the lecture that had changed my life. I knew that I should stick my neck out and argue on Huang's behalf. Nevertheless, under the political climate of the day, known as the White Terror, I would have to consider my family's safety. Therefore, I told Chang Teh-ming that I would have to listen first to what my senior alumni and my family had to say.

The atmosphere at the time was rife with terror, as if everywhere we were surrounded by enemies. Instinctively trying to protect me, my senior alumni leaned toward opposing my involvement and asked that I give it more thought. On the other hand, it was Shu-chen, upon hearing the news over the phone, who expressed her support right away. She said, "You know very well that they're not guilty of sedition, yet that's what it's been said they have done. They'll get the death sentence for that. If you don't even have the guts to take a case like this, what good

---

[8] As of this writing, Chen Chu is director of the Kaohsiung City Bureau of Social Affairs.

are you as a lawyer?"

I purposely told her that, if I took this case, it would affect my career as an attorney, yet she still said 'that's okay,' and that if it resulted in a loss of business and a reduction in income, she would gladly accept the consequences.

Pleased that my wife and I were on the very same wavelength, I took the case.Later on, Huang Tien-fu (Huang Hsin-chieh's younger brother) came to see me about completing the retainment of services procedures, and I officially became Huang Hsin-chieh's defense attorney.

Life can be amazing when you think about it. The two turning points in my life thus far were connected to Huang Hsin-chieh. My association with politics and my career turn toward politics both originated in that time.

Previously, I had known little about the opposition movement, but in the process of defending Huang Hsin-chieh and working through the related files I was able to glean information about Taiwan's democracy movement. At first, I approached this case from a professional standpoint as a lawyer. As expected, in the end we lost the case, but never did I anticipate such a heavy sentence. I felt wronged and completely frustrated.

Later, we defense lawyers got together with Frank Hsieh and Su Chen-chang [9] to give some thought to how to handle the situation. This period of contact with some of the players allowed me to become familiar with the Taiwanese democracy movement, and I became deeply moved by the opposition's power. I knew that the best defense is not a tangible court of law, but rather an invisible "court of the people's conscience." **The best defense is not making appeals or requesting re-trials according to legal procedure; on the contrary, the best defense is to continue on the road of democracy that the forerunners of democracy never completed!**

One day in 1981, just before the fourth popular election of Taipei City Council members, I ran into Su Chen-chang on the street. He exhorted me, "A-Bian, let's go for it together!" He was going to run for the Provincial Assembly, while, Frank Hsieh, Lin Cheng-chieh and I would form a united front and run for seats on the Taipei City Council. We would soon become known as the "Three Musketeers."

I had zero preparation coming into the election, as there was only a little more than a month between kicking off the campaign and getting elected. For the longest time we were unable to find a single place within the Sungshan district willing to rent us space for our campaign headquarters. Finally, we found a location on Sungshan Road.

Huang Tien-fu and his wife, Lan Mei-chin (current DPP Taipei City Council member) helped out at our headquarters. Their political pedigree, both having grown up in political households, equipped them to handle all campaign publicity. For lack of a better description, my

---

[9] At this writing, Frank Hsieh (Hsieh Chang-ting) is mayor of Kaohsiung, and Su Chen-chang is magistrate of Taipei County.

wife served as campaign manager. Lacking all experience, I was a bit lost in front of a crowd of people. Sitting in the audience years before listening to Huang Hsin-chieh's speech, little could I have suspected that I would accept the baton of the democracy movement in Taiwan.

Unexpectedly, thanks to popular support for the democracy movement, more and more listeners came to hear me speak, boosting my confidence. Jaw Shaw-kong, competing in the same district as me, cried out "Kramer vs. Kramer" and "elder alumni teaches his younger alumni a lesson," heightening the tension of the election atmosphere. When the results came in, I was elected Taipei City councilman, garnering the highest number of votes.

This was my first step into politics. As a city councilman, my trenchant style and exposure of various government abuses gave the KMT constant headaches. For this I would pay the price of a jail term.

In 1984, *Formosa* magazine published an article on Feng Hu-hsiang's university professor qualification thesis, "Neo-Marxist Criticism," alleging that the thesis appeared to be a case of "translation in lieu of original writing." Feng Hu-hsiang [10] sued me, as director of *Formosa* magazine, for libel. In an effort to settle the matter, the North American Association of Taiwanese Professors enlisted seven professors, including Tien Hung-mao (current director of the Institute for National Policy Research, Chang Fu-mei, Hsiao Hsin-yi, Hsiao Sheng-tieh, Parris Chang, Lin Tsung-kuang, and Lin Tien-min, to

---

[10] As of this writing, Feng Hu-hsiang is a New Party legislator and vice-presidential candidate on his party's ticket.

assess the essay's authenticity. Their assessment read, "Without difficulty, we have reached the unanimous conclusion that Mr. Feng plagiarized the work of others." Nevertheless, on 12 January 1985, the Taipei District Court sentenced defendants Chen Shui-bian, Huang Tien-fu, and Lee Yi-yang to one year of imprisonment each, plus NT$2 million in civil reparations.

On 18 January 1985, I resigned from my seat in the Taipei City Council, announced my refusal to appeal, in protest of unfair justice, and prepared to go to prison. On 8 September of the same year, I was collectively nominated by the *dang wai* [11] to run for magistrate of Tainan County.

The decision to run in this election would ultimately put my wife in a wheelchair, paralyzed from the waist down, for the rest of her life.

On 15 November 1985, my mother-in-law, Wu Wang Hsia, received a threatening letter, claiming that "we're going to put A-Bian's family through the torture of losing a family member and a wife." At first, we treated this as a device intended to cow us and weaken our resolve. After all, in those days, what participant in the *dang wai* democracy movement didn't receive threats? For such reasons, we dismissed the seriousness of the threat.

---

[11] *Dang wai,* literally "outside the party," is a general term describing the opposition movement prior to the founding of opposition parties beyond the ruling Kuomintang (KMT).

Despite the "A-Bian whirlwind" that whipped through Tainan County during the magistrate election campaign, with our rallies attracting tens of thousands of supporters and putting fear into the KMT, in the end we lost the fight. On 16 November 1985, I was defeated by a narrow margin.

On November 18, I led over 100 supporters through the streets of Tainan County to thank voters for their support. As the procession reached the vicinity of Kuanmiao Township, just as we were about to enter the restaurant at which we had arranged for a meal, a three-wheeled "iron ox" car sped into the alley, knocking down my wife.

Just as my wife turned to yell at the reckless driver, the car unexpectedly backed up, ran her over again, then fled the scene.

I haven't the heart to recount the judicial process we endured in the wake of the "accident," except to say that the district attorney's treatment of the case violated all principles of law to an incredible degree. My wife suffered over 30 fractures of the seventh cervical vertebra. After two major surgeries, her life was just barely spared, but paralysis from the waist down has been her fate ever since.

En route to Fengchia Hospital, my wife asked, "Am I going to die? What will happen to the children if I die?"

My involvement in politics took a devastating toll on my wife. She has no feeling below the chest, and since she is unable to perspire, her bodily thermostat is completely off kilter. In addition, elimination of waste is a constant source of agony.

In the days that have followed that fateful day, sometimes I push her wheelchair, or take her to have her hair washed. Standing behind her, I always have the same thought: Why did it have to be she who was hit, and not me? Does my family have to suffer the consequences of my involvement in politics? I think back to over a decade ago, the first time I ran for office. Su Chen-chang said," Let's go for it together!" The words "go for it" in Taiwanese convey a passion that says no turning back —that one is prepared to make the bet of a lifetime and dive in head first. To us, it meant that we were going to change the face of politics! Perhaps we'd go to prison, and maybe someone would take revenge on us. Aware of the stakes, we still decided to "go for it." But never in my wildest dreams did I imagine that the one to pay the price would be my wife.

Back then I thought, ' Does politics have to be like this? Shouldn't we have the freedom to speak out, personal safety, and human rights?' I wasn't satisfied!

All these years, I have taken Shu-chen along with me to many major public occasions. There has always been a minority of those who assume that I am using her to win sympathy. But they don't know that I appear together with Shu-chen because we have always walked together in politics. We are a true unit of shared destiny, and in that sense my honor and my setbacks are hers, too.

During her stint as a legislator, the Legislative Yuan lacked facilities for the handicapped. Not only wasn't the Legislative Yuan free from barriers, but no one in charge would even agree to removing the armrests of a seat for her use, saying it would "create an eyesore."

For her entire three-year term, without a seat, she was a legislator in a wheelchair parked in the aisle. During my stay in jail, my wife relied on Yu Cheng-hsien, current Kaohsiung County magistrate and then legislator, to push her around constantly from one session to the next. I'll never forget the compassion and care he showed for a fellow comrade during that time.

On countless occasions I have seen how those with difficulty getting around due to physical or mental handicaps are threatened by everything around them. Maybe I notice this because of Shu-chen's condition, and putting myself in their shoes I feel great empathy for them. This is why, during my term as mayor of Taipei, I vigorously promoted welfare measures for people with mental or physical disabilities and pushed for barrier-free public spaces. In addition, I am determined to see through judicial reform, in hopes that Taiwan can become a safe place where people can be free of fear, and where people are never again persecuted for their politics.

The road is long. Here's to the attainment of fairness and justice before long!

Chapter Three

From Elected Representative to Administrative Chief

Shu-chen visited me in prison. Paralyzed from the waist down, she fell again and again from the revolving stool, yet concerned that I would worry about her, she forced a cheerful smile. I told her, "Enough of all this. All this pain and suffering, the price of the political prisoner, must end here with us. I want a happy, hopeful society free from fear. Our government must serve the people, not control them." Ever since I started out in politics, whether as a popular representative or an administrative chief, I have always kept this truth in my thoughts.

From jailhouse "lessons in democracy" to the legislature

My wife, Shu-chen, was struck by a car on 18 November 1985. After surgery at Taichung Veteran's General Hospital, once her condition had stabilized she was transferred to Taiwan University Hospital in Taipei. All told, she spent about six months in the hospital with all sorts of tubes in her. We waited for a miracle, but no miracle ever materialized.

I knew that she had encountered this adversity because of my involvement in the pro-democracy opposifion movement. Torn up with guilt, I also feared that she and her family would complain. Yet, throughout everything, neither she nor her family ever uttered a word of blame against me, or ever pleaded with me to get out of politics.

Once, lying in her hospital bed, she told me that in Taiwan's democracy movement if either the husband or wife must sacrifice, she was willing to be the one to do so on my behalf. Comforting me, she said, "I can't make money. You can make money to provide for the children. That you weren't the one to get hurt is a fortunate aspect of this unfortunate situation."

Hearing these words, tears welled up into my eyes as I felt my own insignificance and Shu-chen's courage. Later, when she stepped out and ran for a seat in the legislature as a "pinch-hitter" for me, not only did she never whine to her audiences at any time during the campaign, her campaign was exemplified by determination and courage. Strong Wu Shu-chen made it possible for the "Hopeful, Happy" Chen Shui-Bian who ran several years later in the race for Taipei City mayor.

In 1986, I became director of the Taipei branch of the Dangwai Public Policy Committee. On May 3, in protest of the court's ruling on the Formosa magazine case, my wife resolved to circumnavigate the island by wheelchair in a "one NT dollar per person wheelchair march" of protest. Sometimes, when it comes to pursuit of justice, her commitment and courage exceed mine.

On June 10, I entered prison together with Huang Tien-fu and Lee Yi-yang. Each week during my 246-day term, Shu-chen would faithfully appear for the allotted two visits in spite of her difficulty getting around. In the visiting room she sat on a rotating round stool, with no back support and nothing to keep it from moving. Paralyzed from the waist down and unable to control force and direction, each time the stool rotated she would drop straight down to the ground like a kite with a broken string. Again and again she fell, as I sat on the other side of the glass choking back the tears and hoping that she wouldn't fall again.

In the ensuing years, this scene has replayed in my mind over and over again. I see her weak, pale face and her eyes full of concern and courage, as if she owes me from a past life and in this life is shouldering the burden for me. To have her as my soul mate on the journey of life, I indeed count my blessings. I will also always recall how on the way to Tucheng Detention center in the dark of night, everyone in the car kept silent, as if words could trigger an outpouring of emotions and start the tears fliowing.

After my release from jail, Shu-chen confided to me that every time she came to visit me in prison was exceptionally uncomfortable for her due to her inability to perspire. So exhausting was it that after returning home she would collapse for the entire afternoon. While I was in jail, she went from a candidate for legislator to an elected legislator. And by the time she became legislator Wu Shu-chen, I was almost out of prison.

While serving time, my favorite book was <u>The Story of My Life,</u> by Clarence Darrow. Darrow was the greatest criminal defense lawyer in American history and a humanist on the side of equality. I read the book and contemplated it over and over, and wished that Taiwan would have more people like Darrow.

The Democratic Progressive Party was officially founded on 18 September 1986. Unable to join in the celebrations from jail, I was nevertheless full of joy. How many fighters had sacrificed in the past, and now an opposition party, a supervisory force, had finally been established.

Following my release from prison on 10 February 1987, I became legislator Wu Shu-chen's special assistant. In the interest of professionalism and efficiency, I led the way to establish the first legislator's office with 14 aides. I began to learn how to write an interpolation query, while we enlisted Lee Yi-yang to handle the writing of our general interpolation documents.

We touched on a wide range of issues during interpolation sessions including national defense, finance and economics, constitutional government, judicature, and cross-strait relations with China. I also studied hard to arm myself with all kinds of knowledge and maximize our professionalism. For specialized issues, we sought qualified professional aides to handle the writing.

Later, we brought in a number of young, professionally trained individuals as staff aides. Securing talent and dividing tasks, we were equipped to contribute to the modern trend toward specialization in politics. Modern politics is not a battleground for heroes; rather, it requires the formation of teams to realize truly efficient specialized operation. I let this approach guide me throughout my career leading to entering the mayor's office, where I treated the organization of the city government team as job one. As a legislator back then, however, the congress only provided staff salary for one aide, which led us to establish the Formosa Foundation to cultivate and support congressional aides.

In December 1989 I was elected as one of the last to join the legislature in supplementary elections, preceding the retirement of the "senior legislators" elected back in China in the 1940s. After taking office in 1990, I served as the DPP party caucus whip. At the time, the DPP had over 20 legislators in the congress, and by 1992 when I succeeded at re-election, our number had grown to over 50 legislators. From special aide to my wife, to becoming a legislator in my own right, my approximately eight-year tenure in congress coincided with a period during which the Legislative Yuan became the center of Taiwan's politics.

The years I spent in the Legislative Yuan account for some of my most cherished experiences. I was fortunate to serve as the Democratic Progressive Party's first Legislative Yuan party whip, thereby stepping into the media spotlight. In the legislature, the entire DPP party caucus exhibited quality work and forceful supervision. Within a half year, press reporters and other social groups ranked me as the top legislator.

In addition to acting as a mouthpiece of the people and monitoring the government, I began to give thought to government operation and reform.

During my tenure in the Legislative Yuan, I championed the Legislative Yuan Organic Law, proposing that each legislator should have at least four congressional aides funded by the state. I succeeded in getting this proposition accepted. Further, a party caucus office is necessary to enhance the function of party caucus operation. Thanks to our concerted efforts, we finally realized this demand as well. For the Kuomintang, a party flush with money, this was never much of a concern; however, for opposition parties, enhancing the tools available to legislators and improving the overall environment is integral to raising the quality of performance in the legislature.

Furthermore, we promoted change in the interpolation system, forcing officials to confront questions directly rather than skirting around the issues. Moreover, approaches that we championed, such as "legislator specialization" and "legislative session political party operation," gradually became reality.

Aiming to become a specialized legislator, I published two

national defense position papers over the years, "The Black Box of Defense" and "The Art of War into the Next Century," each offering in-depth investigation of defense policy and management. As a specialist in defense issues, I exposed numerous abuses within the military while devoting thought to mapping out the future of national defense and security.

At first, when it came to the substantive operational approach of the Legislative Yuan, two cases had the greatest impact. In fact, they can be considered watershed cases in the course of Taiwanese democratic reform. The first such case was the repeal of Article 100 of the Penal Code in 1990, shortly after I entered the legislature. This article attracted our attentions since between the first client I had defended a decade earlier as an attorney, Huang Hsin-chieh, to my most recent client, Hsu Hsin-liang, there had been innumerable similar cases —all tied to Article 100 of the Penal Code!

In my view, the crucial issue was not the "Temporary Provisions Effective During the Period of Communist Rebellion," which governed penalization of sedition, but the repeal of the mother law —Article 100 —upon which it was based. Article 100 laid down the parameters of "regular treason," but the text of Section Two read: "Criminals guilty of intent, or conspiring to violate the previous section, shall be sentenced to a period of incarceration between six months and five years." In this way, "thought" could constitute criminal behavior, so that even dreaming could be construed as sedition. Thus, such a nebulous idea of law gave authorities complete license to find anyone guilty, so that law became a semantic prison wielded by authorities to avenge or attack dissenters. Article 100 allowed the creation of "thought criminals," so that as long as it was not revoked, there would always be thought criminals and a "black list" of persona non grata.

We subsequently pushed for the repeal of Article 100, so that gradually it became a focal point of political attention. Establishing consensus throughout society ensured that, even after the repeal of the "Temporary Provisions Effective During the Period of Communist Rebellion," the KMT remained under pressure. Joining the "100 Action Alliance" composed of members of the medical and academic communities, we saw to it that even Ma Ying-jeou wouldn't touch the article with a ten-foot pole. In the end, the "untouchable" Article 100 was repealed, finally safeguarding the constitutional right of all Taiwanese to freedom of thought.

The other vital case is the full retirement of the "senior" legislators and national assemblymen elected in China. Despite the existence of Voluntary Retirement Provisions, they stubbornly resisted mere moral solicitation, preventing the infusion of new blood into the congress. Clearly, it was too much to ask of the old congressmen to raise their hands and cast their vote to eliminate their own political stage and influence.

In order to effect a fundamental change in the "congress pickled in formaldehyde," it was necessary to step beyond traditional thinking and elevate strategy to the constitutional level. With this in mind, I submitted the No. 261 Constitutional Interpretation Bill in March 1990. In alliance with different factions, including the more enlightened members of the KMT, we submitted an appeal to the Grand Justice to interpret the constitution. On June 21, learning that the constitutional interpretation bill had passed, I was overcome with joy. Without the No. 261 Constitution Interpretation Bill, there could not be election anew of the national congress, nor would we have today's democratic reform and progress!

In addition to these two political reforms, my decision to concentrate on the field of national defense put me up against a great deal of difficulty. Back then, legislators whose mission it was to represent the interests of the military completely ran the military subcommittee in the Legislative Yuan. With them in control, an "outsider" could never butt in to cut even a penny from the budget, or question the rationality of the military budget without being branded "unpatriotic." Having such a dubious label cast upon one's head made it impossible to get anything accomplished.

Setting my goals, I proposed a four-pronged platform for defense reform: nationalization of the military, legal dominion over security and intelligence organs, alignment of military administration and military directives, and open operation of military procurement. In order to achieve these ideals, I not only had to join the military subcommittee, but I must have the chance to act as its convener. After prolonged and concerted effort, I finally got my wish and assumed the role of military subcommittee convener in March 1992.

Over the process of transformation of national defense, we promoted a draft bill of the National Defense Organic Law. Following thorough discussions with representatives of various fields, the Legislative Yuan finally began to review the bill in October 1999.

In order to develop new cross-strait relations founded on peace, parity, mutual benefit, and cooperation, I proposed a "Foundation Draft Treaty Between the Republic of China and the People's Republic of China" in the attempt to go beyond the confines of traditional thinking and clear a path for Taiwan's future. For me, the entire process of serving as a legislator was one of learning about national security and promoting human rights and democratic reform. Despite the demanding nature of these tasks, it was nonetheless worth every effort, as I had the good fortune, along with other like-minded people, to be right in the middle of major progress in an era of change in Taiwan.

When I think of it, the path of a popularly elected representative cannot be taken alone; rather, it requires the collection of wisdom. I acted as a conduit, expressing this wisdom to others. This was my main achievement as a legislator. On Taiwan's road to democracy, people power has always moved ahead of the government. Finally, bottom-to-top power generated political reform. It was this force that pulled me into politics and made me become a people's representative. Similarly, it was this force, translated through votes, that took me to the mayor's office to work on behalf of the people of Taipei.

First campaign for mayor of Taipei

In August 1993, I began preparing to run in the first race for mayor of Taipei elected directly by popular vote, to be held in December 1994. At the same time, the positions of mayor of Kaohsiung City and governor of Taiwan Province were also up for direct popular election. Determined to run for mayor of Taipei, I established the Chen Shui-Bian Municipal Administration Center. I knew the Kuomintang had money and manpower, and that if we were to win the battle we needed to rely on more than notoriety; we must definitively map out our administrative program for Taipei, and get to know the needs of the city's citizenry.

In April 1994, working together with 18 scholars and experts, the Chen Shui-Bian Municipal Administration Center unveiled a book entitled <u>18 Transformations for the Taipei Metropolis</u>, formally demonstrating our understanding of Taipei, and how our plans and imagination applied to the governance of Taiwan's capital city.

On July 17, at the conclusion of the first stage of the Democratic Progressive Party nomination primary, I led Frank Hsieh by 957 votes.

In days gone by, Frank Hsieh and I had both worked as defense lawyers for the defendants in the Kaohsiung Incident. Later in that same year, we ran for city councilman and launched our respective political careers together. After all these years, we were still giving our all, striving for the ideals summed up in the momentous exhortation to "Go for it!"

I am grateful to Frank Hsieh, not only for stepping aside in the interest of party unity before the second round of the party primary, but also for agreeing to serve as my campaign manager. My mentor, constitutional law authority Lee Hung-hsi, also contributed everything he had in assistance.

I hoped to run a different kind of campaign. I also hoped for the chance to become mayor of Taipei, and to forge Taipei into a gleaming, cheerful, and hopeful city.

Never did I expect that the mayoral race would stir the strongest ethnic tensions ever in Taiwanese political history.

Three candidates competed for the mayor's seat, myself representing the DPP, Huang Ta-chou representing the KMT, and Jaw Shaw-kong representing the New Party. Looking back, it was truly an intense race.

Not only was it a competition of political platforms, but a struggle of ethnic consciousness. The intensity of the atmosphere was such that it put the entire city of Taipei on the brink of a pressure cooker. The tension only intensified when Jaw Shaw-kong accused President Lee Teng-hui of having an "urgent timetable for Taiwan independence."

Back then, the DPP was often smeared as a "violent party" that went around creating conflict. Naturally, we didn't want to stir up conflict during the election. Taipei is a city bursting with potential. **We wanted Taipei to have the chance to regenerate into a civilized, efficient, happy city.**

The campaign slogan "Cheerful, Hopeful, Chen Shui-Bian" evoked the philosophy of "Taipei —The New Hometown." In other words, it symbolized the hope that everyone, regardless of ethnic heritage or party affiliation, might live together in peace. Amidst this mild atmosphere, we garnered over 615,000 votes, or 43.6% of the vote, ahead of second-place Jaw Shaw-kong, with 420,000 (30%)

votes.

That night at our campaign headquarters, looking over the rapturous, dancing crowd, I was both elated and solemn. Thinking about my journey in politics, I had made the transformation from a watchdog to an implementer of policy. In this role, I must plan out municipal administration, holding nothing back. I was truly happy to have the chance to serve as mayor of Taipei, and I made a solemn promise to myself to build Taipei into a safe and happy city.

My young staff members, such as Ma Yong-cheng, Luo Wen-jia, Lin Jin-chang, and Lin De-xun, as well as my entire office of congressional aides, achieved victory with a fresh kind of campaign. Despite our lopsided disadvantage in terms of resources, our ability to win credibility with the city's citizenry can be attributed to our entire team's spirited morale, vigor, and not least, our concrete platform for reforming city administration.

Taiwan is a stress-filled society where everyone tends to put ideological considerations ahead of all else. Ethnic issues are especially sensitive and serious, often playing with people's minds and transforming into collective fear and anxiety.

I failed to win the trust of all ethnic groups in the second mayoral election. Following my defeat, I reflected deeply on this issue: where had I gone wrong? What had I said or done that struck fear in some people? What direction should Taiwan take? These happened to be the issues I reflected upon the most concerning Taiwan, which subsequently led me to propose the "New Middle Road," designed to transcend ethnicity and party affiliation, and to put national security at its core.

The new city government's "conceptual revolution"

When I had the opportunity to begin serving in the Taipei City government on 25 December 1994, the Taipei I headed as mayor was congested with traffic, chaotic and dirty, shot through with prostitution and illegal video and gambling game parlors. It was the home of the most expensive mass rapid transit railway the world had seen —yet frequent episodes of "spontaneous combustion" made completion and regular operation far beyond the distant horizon.

I proposed a platform for the New City Government Movement centering on our 1-2-3 Action Plan. In addition, I emphasized the underlying principle that "city administration will not settle for anything less than 100 percent, nor will it take kickbacks," as we were determined to forge a clean, capable, and efficient city government. The 1-2-3 Action Plan consisted of the one principle of civil orientation and civil participation; the dual strengthening of cultural and recreational activities and social welfare for Taipei citizens; and priority promotion of educational reform, traffic reform, and reformation of urban development.

"In a state of disrepair, awaiting full-scale reconstruction." That is the only way to describe Taipei at that time. Previously, I had visited a number of different countries and cities, each time stirring up a great deal of feelings. In Japan, Singapore, Europe, or America, I would think of Taiwan, contemplate Taipei: when it came to historical preservation, we had none; when it came to modernization, we weren't far enough. The people in these places I visited were so orderly, spaces were so clean, and residents enjoyed such civilized, comfortable environments. Unquestionably, we could not measure up. This is why I have always felt that once a citizen has food on the table and clothes on his back, he should try to make some time to give to the public. It was with this in mind that I proposed the concept of a "volunteer Taiwan" after the devastating 21 September 1999 earthquake. To change Taipei and transform Taiwan will require the participation of all our citizens.

As a Taipei City councilman or national legislator, this philosophy fueled my desire to engage in maximum supervision of public interests. Still, a watchdog's possibilities are limited, and the role kept me far away from the ideal vision I kept in my mind. This is why, given the chance to enter an administrative department, I knew that this was it! This was my chance to put the concern and urgency I had felt for so long into action.

I kept wondering, 'Taipei City has so many resources, and the highest caliber civil servants in the country, why then does the administration seem so lethargic?' I recalled how my predecessor, Mayor Huang Ta-chou had remarked privately to me that improving the traffic situation in Taipei was practically impossible —unless industry were hit by a major depression or there were a serious population exodus.

I knew that our first task in City Hall was to undertake a

"conceptual revolution."

I sought to forge a service-oriented, goal-oriented, vigorous government. Civil servants must understand and appreciate that they are the "servants of public interest," that the public takes precedence over the individual, and that service cannot be denied. The most important reason preventing the resolution of Taipei's lethargy and disorder was a conceptual issue.

Shortly after taking office, I presented each level-one supervisor with a copy of the book <u>Raving Fans: A Revolutionary Approach to Customer Service,</u> by Kenneth H. Blanchard. My intentions were simple: a government should be like a corporation since it is a service undertaking, not a monopoly that can settle for standing still. I asked colleagues in the city government to think of the city's citizens as customers. We needed to provide the most comprehensive, most responsive service on all fronts.

The first step towards change would naturally cause a bit of discomfort, but the vast majority of city government civil servants are possessed of talent, vision, and self-esteem. Drawing on these qualities, in our four years in office we were able to realize the Taipei experience that exemplifies the DPP's party slogan: "green[12] administration —the quality guarantee."

---

[12] Not to be confused with the world's various Green Parties, the DPP party colors are green and white.

The four-year "Taipei Experience"

Although those of us in the Taipei City government served for just a short four-year term, we exacted precise plans, administered them diligently, and accomplished numerous "missions impossible." This "Taipei Experience" gave me confidence to renew the government.

I made the first step toward this conceptual transformation on the front line of civil service —the city's district offices and housing administration offices. Previously, the counters were 120 cm. high, forcing citizens to remain standing while seeing to their business. The excessively high counters created distance and an overbearing, authoritative impression, as if a Berlin Wall separated the city government and Taipei's people. I told my colleagues in the city government: "The government exists for the people; without the people there is no government. From today forward, we shall lower the counters, make all work open and transparent. Most importantly, we must be on the same level as the people." This was the first step in the conceptual revolution.

Next, we promoted the "complimentary tea" movement. Public servants must treat customers with respect, providing them with the best service. This change (once instituted, a major departure from the torpid exercises in frustration to which they had become accustomed) made Taipei citizens coming in to take care of their business feel pampered.

Next, we collated files, and made all information available on an internal computer network, allowing citizens to go in and out in a jiffy, causing friends and relatives waiting outside to assume they must have forgotten something, since there was no way they could be finished so fast.

Beginning with housing administration, we began promoting a series of courtesy measures, extending them to land, tax, and motor vehicle administration. Thanks to these measures, **Taipei's housing administration agencies were awarded the prestigious honor of ISO9002 quality certification, making ours the first government agency in Asia to receive such certification. This award attracted the notice of Japan's NHK Television, which put together a special report for its Who's Who in Asia program, asking the question "If Taiwan can, why can't Japan?"**

These examples solidify my belief that government transformation must begin with a conceptual revolution. In turn, success or failure depends on how hard people try to see it through.

Further, over our four years in office we advocated "civic participation." In the past, the Kuomintang always played up the notion of a "totalistic government" —encouraging the idea that the government should be relied upon to handle everything, even though it often failed. Therefore, we must admit that government is limited in its capacity, not omnipotent, and that there are some things the government cannot accomplish or simply should not undertake. In other words, it should effectively utilize public resources, while joining with the unlimited power of the private sector, thereby accomplishing infinite things with a finite government.

This is why the city government did its best to partner with private strength in the promotion of many events. Utilizing private funding, planning, and participation, we steadily evaporated the distance between the government and the private sector. Working in such a fashion, over the course of several years people will come to feel as though the government is closely integrated into their lives. This is the way it should be, as the government really belongs to everybody and exists for the people's current lives and future dreams. We brought in numerous volunteers and helpers, who got involved whether we were promoting government administration or events related to culture and the arts. So it is clear that our four-year Taipei Experience blossomed out of the concept and implementation of a "finite government joining with infinite private resources and strength." Examples include the operation of the Wanfang Hospital, the Children's Museum, and down the line to the local level with neighborhood parks, underpasses, pedestrian walkways, and a roadside tree adoption program. Even the "Mosquito Cinema" (free outdoor movie) series, the Taipei Literature Awards, poetry inside public buses, the Taipei Arts Festival, Taipei Lantern Festival, and Taipei Jazz Festival were all boosted by the infinite power of the private sector.

Within four years, the Taipei City government became courteous, accommodating, and efficient. Despite the withdrawal of the French company MATRA, the Taipei Rapid Transit Systems (TRTS) began safe operation, with the augmentation of one line per year —well in advance of schedule. Prostitution and video game parlors, the bane of residential life, were virtually shut down across the board. Traffic conditions were improved beyond recognition. We promoted "youth protection measures," instituting a midnight curfew requiring minors to head home, helping make Taipei a safer city and setting parents' minds at ease. We also focused full attention on women's issues, including women's rights in the workplace and protection of equal rights between the sexes.

We actively promoted social welfare for the needy. In educational reform, we streamlined various admissions procedures, and in urban development issues, we promoted unique community reformation programs.

Four years is a short time, but we worked hard and accomplished a great deal.I recall the first time I made an overseas visit as mayor. The date was 28 February 1995, and I went to Japan to survey how the Japanese had handled restoration efforts in the aftermath of the Osaka-Kobe earthquake. With this experience under my belt, after returning to Taiwan I set about planning for a comprehensive rescue equipment and response system for Taipei.

Summing up our four-year Taipei Experience, in addition to the impact of precise objectives, clear ideas, and robust execution, I am deeply grateful for the contributions of the city government managerial team and staff to our success. Without their care, their determination, their wisdom, and their fortitude, none of this could have been accomplished.

On the eve of the second direct Taipei mayoral election, Taipei City was ranked fifth by the English edition of Asiaweek magazine among the most livable cities in Asia. From ugly duckling to proud swan, it took a lot of work, but we did it!

Chapter Four

Putting Together a Winning Team and Approach for Success

Many members of my miniature city government "cabinet" had never supported me in the past, or had actively opposed me. Nevertheless, seeing eye-to-eye on issues of city administration, they came to appreciate my management philosophy, enabling us to work together for four years in the city government, making the Taipei Experience in Asia the pride of all Taiwanese.

Finding and exploiting people's talents

As mayor, in addition to being a policy-maker regarding administrative philosophy, I also had to play the role of "manager." The two roles went hand-in-hand and success could not come without equal attention to both.

When I began my term of service in the city government, I knew that for the government to transform and progress, we must integrate with people from all walks of life, like a company looking for top-drawer managerial staff.

I took a need-based philosophy to the engagement of talent, blind to ethnic background or party affiliation, putting this philosophy into practice. In the new hometown of Taipei, every member of Taiwan's four major ethnic groups (aborigines, *Fulaoren*, Hakkas, and the various *Waishengren* who arrived in Taiwan with the Nationalist government) is part of Taipei's new generation — regardless when they or their ancestors arrived in Taiwan. The same holds true when applied to the rest of Taiwan in general.

The city government team had five main staff members, including two deputy mayors, one secretary-general, and two deputy secretary-generals. Among the five positions, so-called "mainlanders" held three, while a Hakka and a *Fulaoren* each held one. I believe these facts amply illustrate my approach to employing people's talents.

Getting started in the city government, I knew that we would have to rely heavily on talent from the public sector. This was particularly true when it came to making good on my campaign commitment to improving traffic conditions, where I needed to find the best candidate for the job. This led me to find Ho Cheng-tan, president of a private corporation and member of the KMT. We shared no connections from the past, nor had he supported me in the election. Still, I moved him with my passion for reforming municipal administration and not only did he join our City Hall team, he was instrumental in helping me make good on my promise to "improve traffic conditions in Taipei within two years." During and after the battle for re-election, Ma Ying-jeou singled out Ho as someone he would like to keep for his new administration, yet Ho decided to exit the city government with our administration.

Next was the city government's financial custodian, the director of the Bureau of Finance. Management and apportionment of the entire city government's finances for development depend upon this individual, under whose jurisdiction also lies the crucial Taipei Tax Bureau. I invited Mr. Lin Chuan, director of National Chengchi University's Department of Finance and Taxation, to assume this role. Surprised, he candidly informed me that he had never been my supporter in the past, had never voted for me, and that he could barely speak the Hoklo language (the language spoken by *Fulaoren,* who account for the majority of the population in Taiwan). As for his first concern, I indicated that it was entirely inconsequential. As for his second reservation, it was clear that he feared a "*Benshengren* chauvinism" with a DPP-led administration. I was both saddened by this reservation, and upset at the misunderstandings separating different ethnic groups. I indicated to him that his second reservation was even less warranted. Subsequently, as director of the Taipei City Bureau of Finance, Lin Chuan not only supported City Hall's reformation and social services measures, helping secure a budget increase to NT$170 billion in our last year from NT$140 billion during my predecessor Huang Ta-chou's administration, but he also managed to reduce the city's debt from NT$107.5 billion to about NT$102.9 billion over the same period.

When the chief of the Taipei City Police Department, a *Fulaoren*, left his position in a reshuffling, I disregarded the suggestions of various ranking officials and selected Ting Yuan-chin, a mainlander from Shandong. In Ting's one year as chief of police, I gave full support to police administration and he worked well with us in return, exercising public authority to full effect. He has since moved on to the central government as director-general of the National Police Administration under the Ministry of the Interior, and we maintain excellent contact —not because he served in the city government, but more importantly because he knows that I am a champion of the police administration.

Taipei's rapid transit system not only began as the world's most expensive such network, but a world-class joke. This morass was typified by opposing factions' bitter struggles, the result of deep-seated ills virtually paralyzing the system.

I needed to find an expert in engineering and an expert in management if the Taipei Rapid Transit Systems were to be saved.

Back when I was a legislator, I had faced off with Chen Chao-wei in question-and-answer sessions. Despite our disagreements, I was impressed with his intelligence and professionalism. I had read in the papers that following the privatization of BES Engineering Corporation, Chen had been threatened by organized crime elements and was preparing to leave his post there. Therefore, I picked up the phone and invited him to leap into the fire that was the Taipei City subway system. I told him that the operation of the entire rapid transit system hinged upon three important positions: Department of Rapid Transit Systems, and the chairman and president of the Taipei Rapid Transit Company. With this understanding, he subsequently chose to serve in the Taipei Rapid Transit Company, taking on the dual roles of chairman and president in order to prevent the infighting that had occurred between the previous chairman and president.

However, the Department of Rapid Transit Systems and the Taipei Rapid Transit Company had a history of not getting along, posing a dilemma. What should we do? We needed a good cooperative rapport, so I trusted him to recommend a candidate for Department of Rapid Transit Systems director who could let him put his thoughts into action and devote full efforts to reform. Chen Chao-wei recommended Lin Ling-san, deputy director general of the Industrial Development Bureau. Working closely together, Chen and Lin got the Mucha and Tamsui lines up and running. And thanks to his outstanding performance, Lin Ling-san was recruited by the Ministry of Transportation and Communications to serve as director general of the Directorate General of Rapid Transportation Systems, in charge of rapid transit affairs on a national scale. However, in order to make good on my promise to get the Taipei Rapid Transit Systems' Hsintien and Chungho lines up and running, I asked Director General Lin to continue contributing at his current post. Meanwhile, Chairman Chen Chao-wei was stolen away by the Ministry of Economic Affairs to straighten up the Chinese Petroleum Corporation, a company with a dubious reputation for constant abuses and industrial safety problems. I am extremely proud of the accomplishments of these two appointees.

A further example is the Taipei Water Department. According to long-standing practice, the director of the Taipei Water Department was always held by a "Taiwanese," never by a *Waishengren*. This struck me as quite an unusual tradition. Reform of the water department required strong medicine. After looking over the employee register, then gathering and reviewing related materials, and finally cutting to the chase with interviews, I decided to have Lin Wen-yuan, then serving in the General Engineering Department and a "mainlander," promoted directly to director of the Water Department, sidestepping restrictions on seniority. With this appointment, the Water Department was transformed from a stagnant pool of water into a bubbling spring. Even though water utility rates were never raised a penny over our four years, each year the Water Department exceeded the legally set limit on net profit, as procurement irregularities and fixed bidding were banished into the past. Moreover, the Taipei Water Department maintained amicable relations with the union, and even had enough enthusiasm and energy to establish a water museum.

In addition to thinking beyond the artificial confines of ethnic background and party affiliation, I made even greater effort to promote qualified females. Many female city government department heads or representatives accompanied me to or attended various international conferences on my behalf, distinguishing themselves with their performance and making a deep impression on international attendees.

Thinking back to the establishment of the City Hall team, in addition to Luo Wen-jia, Ma Yong-cheng, and Lin Jin-chang, who brought youth, creativity, and energy to the team, **my approach to personnel is based on the idea of "not using those you doubt, and not doubting those you use." Knowing who is best for the job is the first rule of administration, after which comes attention to cooperation and coordination among various departments.** Not just the individuals mentioned above, but overall the City Hall team was an innovative new administrative team with ideals, goals, methods, and efficiency. Working side by side with me, they helped make Taipei a better, safer place.

One must offer dignity, support, and room for maneuvering in order to allow individuals to make the most of their potential in their position. Only by forging opportunities within the organization does the organization have opportunities. I am grateful to the city government team, for without them there could never have been a new city government boasting a 76% approval rating.

Losing the election made it impossible for the city government team to continue working toward achieving the aims of our blueprint for the city. Nevertheless, in retrospect, ours was a different kind of four years.

The four-point program of "government management"

From people's representative to administrative chief, this shift in roles led me to often invoke the "table theory" to describe my feelings and discoveries.

If popular opinion is a table, elected people's representatives can see just the tabletop without having to look at what's under the table. It is sufficient for them to see just one of the table's four corners, since they often represent a portion of public opinion or special interests, and they can fight for the rights and interests of that segment of the population and be considered a competent people's representative.

On the other hand, an administrative official cannot see only the table top, but must be able to see into the dead ends, dark areas, and blind spots under the table; he must not be kept in the dark, as what is under the table can sometimes be more important than the surface. One example that comes to mind is underground sanitary sewers.

An administrator must be open to opinions from all around and keep various points of view in mind at all times, taking even minority opinion seriously. Still, he cannot accommodate everyone, necessitating choice and the integration of various opinions upon which policy decisions are made and carried out.

I have always believed that turning policy decisions into workable actions requires a concrete approach, strategy, method, and management similar to that applied to the operation of a corporation. Likewise, government management should be enterprise management, based on structure and planning. **I summarize the government management methods applied during our four-year Taipei Experience into four categories of management: goal management, growth management, dynamic management, and crisis management.** It takes four stable legs to stand a table up; similarly, all four management approaches must be used in conjunction with one another to achieve administrative renewal that will ultimately transform a government that in everyone's eyes appears slow to react and out of synch with popular will.

Goal management

Every enterprise has its operational goals, such as fixed production value or profits. Always setting these targets higher, goal management can be considered very well defined. Naturally, government administration cannot lack goals and could stand to learn a few things from business.

For example, when I promised to improve Taipei's traffic conditions within two years, naysayers were everywhere, pointing to the constant growth in the number of people and vehicles in Taipei, plus the fact that work on the rapid transit system had created a "dark age" of bad traffic in the city. Yet two years later, traffic conditions had truly improved. To set and realize such a goal took planning, execution, and constant assessment.

From keeping intersections clear to prevent gridlock, cracking down on violations, opening up bottle necks, establishing exclusive public bus lanes, to completing major transportation projects ahead of schedule posed a juggernaut of challenges, but a unified set of goals.

Shortly after taking office, lacking appropriate funding, we were forced to innovate in other ways, having police officers stand out in traffic, rain or shine, to keep intersections clear and prevent congestion. And while traffic remained tight, we managed to keep it from getting out of control. Further, Ho Cheng-tan, director of the Taipei Bureau of Transportation, told me that in order to improve Taipei's traffic conditions, public bus express lanes were necessary. At first opposition was vocal, so we began with a few select main roads. The previous administration had prepared a public bus lane on Nanking East Road, but caved into vociferous opposition and scuttled the project, wasting money and losing public trust.

Although opposition to the first public bus express lane outweighed support, given its effectiveness we had to stand by the project. Over the next seven months the city government completed seven bus-only express lanes, not only stimulating a rise in the rate of bus utilization, but also improving traffic conditions.

Another example is sanitary waste sewage lines, an important indicator of the national quality of life. According to 1995 statistics, Denmark's sanitary sewage line connection rate was 98%, Switzerland's 91%, with South Korea, the Philippines, and Indonesia each around 40%. Meanwhile, Taiwan showed a paltry 3.4% connection rate, giving it away as a high-income nation with the most unsanitary sewage lines.

Previous city government administrations failed to work on this area. After all, it is not a good way to curry favor and it remains invisible to the eye even when done. When wastewater from countless homes is discharged directly into rivers and streams without channeling or treatment, how can we expect to have clean rivers?

As of 1995, the wastewater drainage line connection rate stood at 3.4% nationwide, approximately 24% in Taipei, about 4% in Kaohsiung, and less than 1% in the rest of greater Taiwan. Having recently assumed office, I knew that working on waste water sewage lines wasn't glamorous, but that it was necessary. If improvements weren't made, Taipei would remain a backward city and Taiwan a backward country in spite of the island's wealth. Setting my target rate at 40%, we went hard after our goal, achieving a 41% connection rate throughout Taipei City by the time I left office.

In 1998, the English edition of Asiaweek magazine called Taipei's improvement the quickest in all of Asia. These accomplishments were all realized with four solid years of effort, enabling Taipei to appear among Fortune magazine's top ten "best cities to do business in Asia" in 1997, in just the third year of the "New City Hall Movement." The next year, our fourth, Taipei ranked fifth among Asiaweek's "most livable cities in Asia."

When it comes to goal management, focusing on what needs work and holding back for nothing are crucial.

Growth management

"Growth management" seems self-explanatory on the surface. We all need growth and pursue growth, but we cannot forget management, because only managed growth is real growth. Aimless pursuit of surface growth, prosperity and progress while forgetting management and controls, can only bring certain disaster.

Shortly after her election as mayor of Hsichih Township, Chou Ya-shu came to see me at City Hall. During our meeting, I reminded her that if Hsichih were to pursue prosperity and progress to the exclusion of all else, paying attention only to surface achievements such as skyscrapers popping up all around and tax revenues increased, the town's residents would eventually be the ones to suffer.

I pointed this out because Hsichih, while pursuing growth, had not paid attention to management. Consequently, as the population grew the infrastructure became inadequate, and basic public works (such as sewage lines) were not put into place. Meanwhile, the education of residents' children also became a problem.

Viewed from the highway, Hsichih looks like a smaller version of Taipei, and in some respects actually appears more modern than Taipei due to the height and appearance of its buildings. Nevertheless, its sewers are uncovered, threatening pedestrians, illustrating that Hsichih's public spaces are not yet fully modernized.

In other towns and cities, such as Tamsui, Pali, or Hsintien, we see closely packed skyscrapers, but has there been any urban planning? The roads are so narrow, even coming to dead ends in some cases. To the government, financial resources seem unlimited, but neglect of growth management and the resulting devastation it brings soon replace the gratification of increased tax revenues.

Some say that for Taipei City, "the bigger the better" should be the rule. On the contrary, I believe that instead of pursuing size, we should seek quality and safety of the living environment. Half of Taipei City sits on hills and mountains, so that in order to increase the city's population it is necessary to fight for land with the hills and nature, damaging soil conservation and the ecology. With this in mind, the new city government proposed hillside development management guidelines prohibiting development on land where the degree of incline exceeds thirty degrees. At first people thought this was too severe, but the Ministry of the Interior soon agreed with this regulation and approach.

Similar to military procurement, isn't it a waste to purchase weapons that are inappropriate or take too much to handle? This is why raising the caliber of personnel, in addition to growth of procurement figures, is a true indicator of military quality and strength.

The "New City Hall Movement" was actually a management movement. We must pursue quality, real growth under sound management.

Dynamic management

Upon entering City Hall, I came to believe that former mayor Huang Ta-chou's description of the city government as suffering from "nerve ending paralysis" didn't go far enough; rather, it was more like congested arteries. Directives from above failed to make it down the chain of command, document culture, formalism, and official culture pervaded. Once I received an official document that had been stamped with over 40 different seals, yet none of those who had stamped it had an opinion. In such cases, once the first person stamped the document, why not send it directly to the mayor's office, instead of wasting the time sending the document around collecting over 40 stamps on an "official document journey?"

Lack of opinions, unwillingness to take responsibility··· if that is how things are, of what use then are all the various official agencies? A and B might express an opinion on an official document, but the next guy has no opinion. Instead, documents are pushed around and around and nothing gets solved.

I asked each unit to have an opinion of its own. Even if it wasn't perfect, at least it represented a given unit's own thinking and sincerity. Many issues call for various relevant units to get together to discuss a solution, so why send documents on such long journeys? A lot of things cannot be resolved while sitting in an office trying to conceive solutions from out of the blue, which is why I hoped that each responsible party would pay a personal visit to understand the situation and the reality of a given issue.

In many cases, sending official documents back and forth takes away time those civil servants should spend serving the people. Instead of working on "essay time," I requested everyone to communicate via fax or orally, accelerating familiarization and effective resolution of problems.

Dynamic management means eliminating official formalities and truly confronting issues. Whether in government or private enterprise, when an organization gets too large the people working inside the organization pay attention to vertical liaison between supervisory and subordinate departments, communicating exclusively with their direct superiors and subordinates. Dynamic management means strengthening horizontal liaisons to link different departments together into a smoothly operating network.

That said, a government capable of "dynamic management" must possess a mechanism with which to raise administrative efficiency, since relying on the mayor, chief of staff, and the heads of various bureaus and departments is not enough. In the case of our new city government, **we looked to the Research, Development and Evaluation Commission (RDEC) to enhance its capacities and function as the heart of the New City Hall Movement.**

The Research, Development and Evaluation Commission must research administrative practice, yet more importantly monitor progress. Dynamic management allows the RDEC to maximize its function as it monitors what each unit is working on, the progress of annual plans, execution of budgets, efficiency, and investigates how improvement can be achieved.

Take for the example the streets of Taipei, which are often dug up, patched over again, and six months later are filled with holes again. Various responsible units are always armed with excuses, but finally the RDEC teamed up with anti-corruption units to survey the real situation, discovering that where regulations dictated that pavement be five centimeters thick, it was only three, and where it should be seven it was only five. Thus the source of frequent road damage was identified: shoddy work and intentional skimping on materials.

As we can see, when the Research, Development and Evaluation Commission carries out its monitoring tasks properly, the New City Hall movement is already halfway to success, for if our watchdog units fail to fulfill their role, capacity and efficiency cannot be maximized no matter how much manpower or budget lies at our disposal.

Pushing aside formality, heading straight to the scene and timely resolution of issues, can contribute to effective handling of horizontal liaison and vertical command, as well as monitoring of progress and efficiency. When integration is possible, departmentalism goes out the window. One good example that comes to mind is the inability of the star-studded Brazilian Football team to defeat the unity and harmony of the French team in the 1998 World Cup.

Only by putting dynamic management to work can prevent working in isolation from happening, and invest government with vitality and efficiency.

Crisis management

When accidents happen, it is necessary to handle the emerging crisis, and if possible to turn the crisis into an opportunity. This, in a nutshell, is what crisis management is all about.

Take for example "preventative defense," which makes active defense the best offense. Similarly, I put a great deal of thought into the promotion of anticipatory municipal administration and preventative management during my term as mayor.

In February 1995, I went abroad for the first time as mayor of Taipei. The purpose of my visit was to survey the damage and understand the restoration efforts following the Osaka-Kobe earthquake in Japan. As the Chinese saying goes, "In peaceful times contemplate danger." Motivated by this knowledge, and knowing that "stones from other hills can serve to polish jade from this one" (one can always learn from the experiences of others), upon my return to Taipei, I immediately took up the task of boosting fire department rescue equipment and training, and systems operation.

Another example of crisis management can be found in the demolition of illegal housing structures occupying the land slated for Taipei's No. 14 and 15 parks. Since nobody had done anything about these structures for half a century, many people ask me why I felt compelled to take action after taking office. Others assume that I couldn't stand to see this corner of the city looking so run-down and thought razing the structures would take care of everything. However, the truth is that given the illegal nature of the structures in the area, relative to established building codes, the building materials and power equipment were fraught with danger. Plus, given the close proximity of households and the crowded conditions, each day I worried about the potentially severe toll of a fire. I believe that the key component of crisis management is to take action immediately upon identifying a potential source of crisis.

Also in 1995, just after I took office, an arsonist set fire to the Ode to Joy KTV parlor, killing 13 in what would prove to be the most deadly fire in Taipei during my term as mayor. At the time we were making preparations for improving public safety measures, and seeing a young person's charred remains taken out of the wreckage was a sobering, heart-wrenching sight. In response, the city government promptly established a Crisis Management Task Force over which I personally presided. Acting according to the principle of "demonstrating sincerity, taking full responsibility," we aimed to handle what needed taking care of. I think that families of the victims appreciated our efforts. In fact, not only did they not blame me or the city government, but they actually presented me and the director of the Bureau of Social Affairs with inscribed plaques, and at the funeral donated NT$300,000 toward public service events funding.

I subsequently worked very hard on public safety issues, taking down many illegal billboards and major illegal structures obstructing escape ways, while also strengthening inspections of fire safety in public places, not hesitating to cut off water and power to offenders in the interest of public safety. During my term in office, the number of fires dropped from around 1340 in 1994 to fewer than 500 in 1997, reducing the corresponding number of deaths from an average of 58 during my predecessor's (Huang Ta-chou) term to 21 per year during my term.

On 25 October 1997, a happy recreational activity took a tragic turn of events when participants in a tug-of-war contest were injured. This is one of the most painful memories of my political career. After learning of the injuries, we quickly arranged for the best medical care for the injured. In addition, that evening Luo Wen-jia, director of the Taipei Department of Information-the event organizer-resigned by way of atonement. I felt particularly guilty and in contrition repeatedly visited and inquired about the victims, while also offering reparation money so as to give both the victims and their families the greatest mental and physical comfort. The Formosa Hope Campaign Rally Troupe actively plugging for DPP candidates for county magistrates and city mayors (other than Taipei and Kaohsiung), also suspended all activities for a week, only resuming once it was clear the injured were out of danger.

Still smarting from the tug-of-war setback, the Formosa Hope Campaign Rally Troupe's first stop after the incident was my hometown of Tainan. There, the locals expressed even greater enthusiasm and support, giving me the confidence necessary to keep going. When the votes were tallied in the election, the DPP collected 43% of the vote, surpassing the KMT for the first time in any election, and claiming 12 of the county magistrate and city mayor positions in Taiwan, thus becoming the majority party on the local level.

The above describes several of my experiences with crisis

management. In addition to resolving crises, crisis management is designed to prevent crises.

Everything the government does affects a wide range of things, touching on a host of issues. **No government that attempts to accomplish things is without its crises,** the only exceptions being authoritarian governments which use crackdowns to suppress the truth of crises and silence dissenting voices. Taiwan has already been through such an era. Today, our politics must move forward, and **all crises must be frankly and openly discussed so as to be resolved through the collective wisdom of many.** Crises are not frightening in and of themselves, but a capable government must utilize maximum efficiency to handle crises whenever they arise.

The above is a sample of my real thoughts, experiences, and philosophy toward government management. Nevertheless, Taiwan's problems are too complex, far exceeding those of Taipei City alone. I am confident that in addition to drawing from one another's experiences, managing the whole from the details up, Taiwan's government reforms must transcend tensions and find a new path. This is why I subsequently contemplated these issues over and over, ultimately proposing my "New Middle Road."

The September 21 earthquake confronted Taiwan with the test of an unprecedented natural disaster. Yet the entire nation's people selflessly reached out in support, offering money and sweat, further affirming for me that this land is fostering hope.

No matter what the circumstances, we all have power. No matter when we arrived, all of us living here are sons and daughters of Taiwan.

Chapter Five

The political philosophy of the New Middle Road

Among *today's international political leaders, I admire British Prime Minister Tony Blair the most. Not only because of his youthful vigor, but more so for the way he as contributed his wisdom and passion to turning hoary old England around, proposing the new approach of the Third Way. Similarly, with the risks and challenges facing Taiwan in mind, I have proposed a New Middle Road for Taiwan, with national security at its core. With this new program, I hope for Taiwan in the new century to stand firmly on the starting line towards ultimate victory in global competition.*

Setting the agenda for the entire citizenry: the key to Taiwanese ascension

On 24 April 1999, NATO's 50th anniversary summit meeting concluded after three days. U.S. President Bill Clinton's discussion of a "third way" with Prime Minister Tony Blair of Great Britain, Chancellor Gerhard Schroder of Germany, Prime Minister Massimo D'Alema of Italy, and Prime Minister Willem Kok of the Netherlands, attracted my undivided attention. The reason is that, ever since stepping down as mayor of Taipei, I have made the "Third Way" an issue of renewed interest and concern.

At the time, I happened to be occupied with a new stage of quiet reflection and study. Seeing how these Western leaders for the time being put aside the crisis in Kosovo and other major global issues to engage in a spirited discussion on political philosophy, exploring how to forge a new path in domestic affairs and economic policy different from the free market or state interference, I was naturally keenly interested.

The Third Way has become a main tenet of political thinking in Europe and America in recent years. How to learn from their new thinking and apply it to political renewal in Taiwan made it a valuable tool of reference. With this in mind, during the spring of 1999, during an interview with the media, I proposed my New Middle Road platform for the first time in public.

Such popular concepts in the 1990s in the West as the Third Way, New Middle Road, or the New Social Contract exemplify the setting of an agenda. While winning two elections in 1992 and 1996, U.S. President Bill Clinton established a new model for setting agendas.

Clinton has been able to successfully set agendas by following a higher level of political philosophy, applying his keen political sensitivity to identify goals, then constantly refining those goals according to public opinion polls. A presidential candidate's mission is to set goals, refine goals, establish goals, then patronize those goals through the media in order to guide the people, stimulating their imaginations and their participation.

Bill Clinton's "agenda revolution" not only took him to the White House once and kept him there for a second term, but has exerted an influence as far as the European Continent. Looking around the European Community, 13 of its 15 member-nations have switched ruling parties during the 1990s, the most notable example being Great Britain's Labour Party, led by Tony Blair, who made a splash with his call for "new Labour, new England." Following 18 years playing second fiddle to the ruling Conservative Party, the Labour Party, led by Blair, took power with a big victory in the May 1997 election. Blair, just 43 at the time, became the youngest British prime minister since 1812.

The British Labour Party's step from minority to ruling party was a great boost of encouragement for the Democratic Progressive Party. Sparking Labour's transformation, and taking stodgy old England on the road to a new life of vigor, Tony Blair can be a model of inspiration for the DPP.

Blair's main appeal to the people was that the Conservatives, after 18 years in power, had become corrupt and devoid of vision; that they were a party run by a minority of individuals unwilling to engage in reform. Blair and Labour insisted that Britain needed new goals, new direction, new leadership, and new identity —the key to which would be tapping into the people's potential to make grand old England young again.

In an effort to wipe away popular stereotypes of the Labour Party, Blair raised the slogan "new Labour, new England," putting a new spin on the socialist dogma the public held in strong suspicion. In particular, the amendment of Article Four of the party's charter put Labour's transformation into action. Blair emphasized that communism had disintegrated, and that socialism is currently merely a moral faith, not the only or best choice for a state mechanism or social system.

With this understanding, Tony Blair abandoned the fundamentalist positions held by the Labour Party throughout the 1980s, proposing the following positions in the revised party platform: maximized effort toward economic and technological development (no longer insisting on state ownership of enterprise), provision of employment opportunities, social welfare structure reform, educational reform, promotion of the "information revolution," and Britain's integration with the European Community. These positions completely changed the face of the Labour Party's image, convincing the people to support Labour's leadership of the government.

Tony Blair's book, <u>New Britain: My Vision of a Young Country,</u>

as well as The <u>Third Way: The Renewal of Social Democracy</u>, by Anthony Giddens, director of the London School of Economics, have given me tremendous stimulation and inspiration, motivating me to raise the New Middle Road as the core thinking of my presidential campaign. Granted, conditions in Taiwan differ from those in Europe and America, and I appreciate that the thoughts and inspiration gleaned from looking to other countries for examples must be translated into a political philosophy tailored to suit Taiwanese society.

With this in mind, I took my time to gather my thoughts before the 10 July 1999 DPP Provisional National Party Delegate Convention, where I formally presented my platform for the New Middle Road as the core philosophy to drive my presidential campaign and to serve as an effective means for Taiwan to succeed in the competitive global arena.

The New Middle Road builds new thinking on top of global vision. The "new individualism" emphasized in this platform goes beyond power, encompassing the duties, responsibilities, and the rights to work and education of the people. Transcending differences of historical background, ethnicity, party affiliation, and opinions on whether Taiwan should unify with or remain independent from China, it aims to take a central political line to establish the largest common denominator among the populace. Engaging in new thinking and new integration rooted in pluralist, inclusive viewpoints, it rejects all extremes. As a matter of course, the New Middle Road focuses on activist groups, non-government organizations, and single-issue organizations, regarding them as important components of the civil society mechanism for achieving cooperation between the public and private sectors. At the same time, it places a premium on the ecology, environmental protection, national land planning, the green revolution, and other issues vital to sustainable national development.

Taiwan's political environment, like Western nations facing the need for development and prosperity, is further plagued with the accumulated ills of the money-mafia political-economic structure, often the fuse igniting internal ideological conflicts. This only convinces us that Taiwan needs a fresh approach to political thinking. More so than Great Britain, Taiwan needs complete transformation. A changing of the guard must take place in Taiwan to enable a fresh new team to lead the restoration of Taiwan. These changes affect Taiwan's future, as well as determine whether Taiwan can compete effectively on the global stage.

The six key objectives of the New Middle Road

Having been strongly affected by the new Western political thinking of The Third Way, on numerous occasions since accepting the DPP's nomination for presidential candidate, I have taken the opportunity to spell out the New Middle Road, and bring up issues according to Taiwan's actual conditions that affect the entire population.

1. Through legislation and administrative approaches, **firmly establish appropriate allotment of power between central and local levels**

of government, and a rational new system for allocation of resources in order to revitalize the local level and enable autonomous local development.

2. **Propose a new platform for constitutional amendments to establish a presidential government system in which power is divided among three bodies** so as to establish a new constitutional government structure ensuring division of power and checks and balances.

3. With global strategy and the security of the Asia Pacific region in mind, **actively practice "risk management" in relation to cross-strait relations** to build popular confidence in the DPP's capacity for government leadership, as well as to safeguard Taiwan's dignity and development.

4. Encourage government, enterprise, and the private sector to establish partnerships, and **fortify the strengths of the civil society to maximize the autonomous vitality of the private sector.**

5. Through local government, police, and community cooperation, **achieve substantive improvements in public safety and establish civic consciousness** so that Taiwanese can live with confidence, a sense of security, and freedom from fear and helplessness.

6. Respond to the challenges of globalization, **placing priority on educational investment and cultivation of intellectual quality,** so that each person has a specialty and a place to apply it, the capacity to compete, and a fine character.

The New Middle Road elicited a great deal of response upon its release to the public. After listening to the opinions of representatives throughout society, **I divided the New Middle Road into six main areas: national security, financial and economic policy, public**

policy, as well as **cultural Taiwan, intellectual Taiwan, and volunteer Taiwan.** I firmly believe that by implementing these six main areas not only can the door be opened to the alternation of political parties, while thoroughly resolving such structural problems as mafia-money alliances, taking Taiwan on a sustainable path forward.

Public confidence in the DPP regarding cross-strait relations has never been high, largely because the DPP has never achieved ruling party status in the central government. Consequently, our expositions on cross-strait relations are not taken seriously, while cast into the prism of the local media, the DPP presidential candidate is forced to bear the burden of public distrust. In my effort to cast off this stereotype, I found inspiration in Tony Blair's new interpretation of Article Four of the Labour Party's platform —sure understanding, plus sincere persuasion, to break beyond the confines of stereotype.

Following close consultation with DPP members from various alliances within the party, as well assorted scholars and experts, I decided to make national security the lynchpin of my New Middle Road platform —a way of thinking that transcends differences on independence vs. unification, ethnic background, or family history. During my visits with political figures while on my "Strategic Security Tour" of the United States and Japan, I constantly underscored the importance of national security, communicating this stance throughout society via the media. After all, **"national security is the lingua franca of all the people"** and the root of Taiwanese survival.

In the early 1990s, following the end of the Cold War, the showdown between East and West had ended on the European

Continent. Meanwhile, despite the collapse of the Soviet Union, China, Japan, the United States, and Russia engaged in a reshuffling of influence in the Asia Pacific region. **As the pieces were reshuffled, the Asia Pacific region developed into three potential flashpoints: the Korean peninsula, the Strait of Taiwan, and the South China Sea. And Taiwan is positioned at the axis of these three major potential flashpoints.**

The United States plays a pivotal role in conflicts around the globe. As the only remaining superpower in the global community, the United States adheres to the strategic aim of "peaceful evolution" in China, in the hope that this strategy will put China under the regulation of the new world order, thereby establishing world peace revolving around the United States.

Consequently, the US Rand Corporation echoes this strategy, suggesting adoption of a containment strategy; on the one hand building a strategic partnership with China, while on the other using military force as a deterrent. The former can be seen in US-Sino bilateral exchanges, while the latter is evident in a deterrent chain established by the US stretching from Japan in the north to as far south as Australia. Situated right in the middle of this deterrent chain, Taiwan's strategic importance speaks for itself.

Looking at this closer, we can appreciate the US's cross-strait policy within its global strategy —to maintain the status quo and stability of Taiwan, keeping Taiwan beyond China's control. Only such a tactic serves America's national interests. The status quo as understood by the United States means not tolerating military encroachment of Taiwan by China, nor allowing Taiwan to declare *de jure* independence. In practice, the United States has a number of options, including safeguarding Taiwan's security and encouraging (but not forcing) Taiwan and China to engage in dialogue and exchange. The legal basis for the former is Article Two of the "Taiwan Relations Act." Concrete actions include dispatching an aircraft carrier to patrol international waters during the 1996 cross-strait crisis, as well as expanding the scope of the "U.S.-Japan Guidelines for Defense Cooperation" to "situations in areas surrounding Japan." Although never defined, the scope of response presumably includes the Taiwan Strait.

The current state of affairs shrouds many complex elements of insecurity. Nevertheless, a pragmatic politician must be able to recognize Taiwan's limitations and opportunities within this strategic framework.

Taiwan's opportunities lie in the importance of its strategic location. If an unfriendly China controls Taiwan, a hole opens up in the US's Asia Pacific regional deterrent chain, forcing it to pull back to Guam and Saipan, or even as far back as distant Hawaii. It is this crucial strategic status that leads the international community (in particular the United States and Japan) to care about and support the freedom and democracy of Taiwan.

That said, in the post-Cold War new world order, the US's new policy of engagement toward China subjects Taiwan's dignity as an independent sovereign state to certain constraints. Clinton's so-called "three-nos policy," and the US claim to not support Taiwan's entry into the United Nations comprise a reality we must understand.

Under the current new global order, Taiwan's security is assured, yet maintaining the dignity of sovereignty is a difficult task. Between the above-mentioned opportunities and restrictions, we must seek a favorable position for Taiwan to stand in the global situation, employing all available tools to improve substantive cross-strait relations.

Turning a new page on cross-strait relations

I'm sure that nobody living in Taiwan wants to see tense cross-strait relations. Moreover, any unsuitable stance or countermeasure can affect future cross-strait developments, especially Taiwan's sustained growth. With this in mind, the peaceful stability of the Taiwan Strait region requires adjusting relations with China, which necessitates understanding China's policy towards Taiwan.

In a word, China's policy towards Taiwan is characterized by unilateral wishful thinking. Disregarding the feelings of the Taiwanese people, it consists of a self-important "one country, two systems" formula. This is applied in a three-phase strategy: 1) The long-term scheme of "peaceful unification, and one country, two systems"; 2) the mid-range tactic of deterring Taiwanese independence; 3) the short-range scheme of pushing for full-scale two-way communications and transportation, and promoting exchange to win over the hearts of the

Taiwanese people.

In actual practice, all measures taken to achieve these three main strategic objectives, seen from a Taiwanese perspective, can be considered belligerent:

1) Militarily, engaging in threats and blackmail, and constant insinuation to the effect that China will not relinquish the use of force to resolve the "Taiwan problem"; this is conducted via military exercises and threats communicated via the media.
2) Diplomatically, strangling Taiwan in order to make cross-strait issues into China's internal affair.
3) Economically, full-scale economic exchange intended to make Taiwan highly dependent upon China. This is designed so that the private sector puts pressure on the government, and commercial pressure overrides political concerns, after which China can secure Taiwan according to the "Hong Kong model."
4) Using cross-strait official interaction, to push Taiwan to accept the "one China principle," so as to eat away the foundation of Taiwanese sovereignty.
5) In covert operations, to recruit sympathizers and divide Taiwan internally, exploiting various contradictions to weaken Taiwan's internal unity.

Following President Lee Teng-hui's statement defining cross-strait relations as "special state-to-state relations," PRC State President Jiang Zemin even went so far as to proffer two conditions for the two sides to resume dialogue: first, retraction of the "two states" position; second, Lee Teng-hui may only receive Wang Daohan, director of the

PRC's ARATS (Association for Relations Across the Taiwan Strait), in his capacity as chairman of the Kuomintang.

Clearly, the leaders of Beijing's Zhongnanhai are still stuck in old thinking. They think that current cross-strait relations are a continuation of the Chinese civil war between the forces of the Communist Party and Kuomintang (Nationalist Party), and that any newly elected president might accept Jiang Zemin's two conditions and continue to engage in negotiations and dialogue with Beijing. But let's be reasonable and consider the situation for a moment. China is still stuck in the past, and incapable of reading the hearts and minds of the Taiwanese people, China resorts to threats in lieu of good will, so how can it be expected to win over the Taiwanese people?

At the same time, we have the above-mentioned understanding and appreciation of global tactics, Asia Pacific regional strategy, and triangular relations among the US, China, and Taiwan, so despite Lee Teng-hui's "special state-to-state relationship" position, China cannot heedlessly take military action against Taiwan in the global climate. This demonstrates that China is bound by the international situation, and cannot afford to act rashly under the new order. That said, Taiwan can ill afford to assume that temporary peace means it can sit back and relax. On the contrary, China has turned to "gnawing away " at Taiwan, rather than trying to swallow it whole. This also happens to be why I constantly underscore that the main tenet of the New Middle Road is national security.

Furthermore, I believe that as long as Taiwan chooses to let the DPP take power in the 2000 presidential election, we can achieve a breakthrough in the old "Chinese civil war" paradigm. The Democratic Progressive Party, a local Taiwanese party produced from bottom to top, having no historical ties to the Chinese civil war, and with the powerful support of popular opinion on its side, can forge a healthy, all-new interactive mechanism across the strait. This is also why I believe that the local DPP must be in power for there to be any hope for the true resolution of the cross-strait crisis. This is also the background to my China Policy White Paper.

From experience, we have learned that cross-strait relations and pragmatic diplomacy are both tools of national policy; neither is more important or urgent than the other. In order to make room for Taiwan's survival, cross-strait relations and pragmatic diplomacy are both levers.

So that Taiwan can go out to meet the world, during my term as mayor I promoted city diplomacy. My visits to the United States and Japan since leaving office have been manifestations of the above-mentioned faith.

Acting out of the philosophy detailed above, on 20 September 1999 I formally unveiled the thoughts I have gathered from long-term investigation and close attention to China policy, proposing the following:

1. We welcome discussion (with China) on any issue.
2. We hope to establish a systemic model for visits and dialogue between Taiwan and China. If obstacles block current channels of discussion, we do not rule out the use of other avenues of communication; whether second or third track, as long as it can help

move dialogue forward, it is welcome.

3. We hope to reduce the risk of military conflict through military mutual-assurance mechanisms. Beginning with such measures as two-way personnel visitation, advance notification of military exercises, sea rescue, and establishment of a hotline, we can gradually reduce hostility and enhance mutual trust.

4. Where national security is not compromised, we propose reviewing and evaluating the lifting of restrictions on direct air links, commercial relations, and investment.

5. Under the condition that China recognizes our equal status as a state, abides by the United Nations' principles for "peaceful resolution of conflicts," and does not presume a set direction for future relations, we advocate signing a peace agreement or foundation agreement as the basis for temporary regulation of cross-strait relations.

Shortly thereafter, I stated that if I am elected president in 2000, I hope to visit China before taking office, and open a new page on normalization of cross-strait relations on the cusp of the new millennium.

I will use the forum of the presidential campaign to raise issues for Taiwan's ascendancy, shattering the lack of issues and mudslinging that has characterized past elections in Taiwan. I hope that we can make use of issues to form consensus among the people, and that my New Middle Road, upon eliciting everyone's acceptance and involvement, can be translated into a blueprint for future administrations, and help engender a final resolution of the knotty and divisive Chinese civil war that has lingered for so long. Fortified by the will of the people and using all the tools at our disposal, we will ask the decision makers in Zhongnanhai to face up to the historical truth and unfold new cross-strait relations based on equality and mutual benefit. This way, on the eve of the new millennium, the people on both sides of the strait can complete preparation for ascent, rather than waste time with hostility. Together, China and Taiwan must forge a win-win situation for the future.

The new DPP's new thinking

While envisioning a cross-strait policy, I exchanged views with countless individuals inside and outside of the DPP and carefully contemplated all that we discussed. This has led me to discover many fresh ways of thinking worthy of further investigation. As examples, Taoyuan County Magistrate Annette Lu's discourse on women's issues, Taiwan's future, and the global situation have brought me considerable edification. Her views have helped me to see that we must aggressively bring together government, private sector, and international strength. We need to communicate on the same plane, and engage in patient persuasion to expand China's disposition to establish friendly relations with Taiwan rooted in peace, mutual trust, and equality. This approach is inspired by the unique female qualities of empathetic communication, patient persuasion, peaceful mutual trust, and equality, to compensate for the cold male severity of the political world.

With this in mind, it is clear that the role of women in Taiwanese society demands aggressive transformation. Taking female involvement in politics, for example, during the era in which my wife, Shu-chen, was involved in politics, many women ran for public office in place of their imprisoned husbands. This history represents the common experience of women in politics in the previous era. Today, it heartens me to see that women are now able to get into politics for themselves —no longer just for the man behind them. Moreover, they can now take issues with which they identify, such as women's issues, environmental issues, and arts and culture to the table, expanding the space and vision of politics so that politics goes beyond raw power   struggle. During my term as mayor of Taipei, I asked National Assembly member Chang Fu-mei and law professor Liu Chu-chih to join my mini cabinet. With Chang in charge of the Commission for Examining Petitions & Appeals, and Liu heading the Civil Servant Training Center, they achieved spectacular results. Women in charge of various city government agencies, such as director Chen Chu of the Department of Social Affairs, director Liu Shih-fang of the Bureau of Environmental Protection, and director Kuo Yao-chi of the Department of Public Housing, even more effectively applied the characteristic attention and care of women in the promotion of their tasks to great effect.

While improvement has been made in female involvement in politics, the problems women face in general in daily life have not been resolved. I think back to just after Shu-chen and I were married, starting our own little family, and how hard it was then. And today, 20 years hence, I'm sure that it hasn't gotten much easier for women. Most people still believe that taking care of children is a woman's work or you must make enough money to pay for expensive day care costs. Other tasks, such as general household work, taking care of the elderly, or even the handicapped, still tend to fall on women.

Having entered the 21st century, the state should find ways to lighten the burden of women, while providing opportunities for women —who account for half the population —to participate in society, freeing their desires and intellect and developing their unique potential. The burden of giving birth and nurturing children is not just the responsibility of an individual or a single family, but should also be the responsibility of society and the state. Our program for the new century must be able to provide a new social structure to enable women to free their desires and intellect and discover their potential. This way, women can better strike a balance between work and family, while society and nation benefit from having a new population of healthy and the active people.

Generally speaking, one of the objectives of the New Middle Road is to cultivate a population of confident women, no longer restricted by male household head authority, and able to fulfill their potential and contribute their talents to helping Taiwan enter the ranks of developed nations and become a country that thoroughly respects women.

In addition to the all-new women's issues detailed above, recently the Democratic Progressive Party has raised a series of varied issues, stimulating broad discussion throughout society. Still, I must emphasize that these issues represent just a small step forward for the new DPP; in the future we will raise more policy issues and demonstrate the new thinking of the "new DPP."

What is the new DPP? In the process of promoting Taiwanese democratization, the DPP initially completed the national identity phase and embarked upon the national construction phase, and is now ready to enter the social construction phase.

With this in mind, we will approach major national policies with a pragmatic eye, thinking outside the boundaries of ideology to confront issues directly. Not a party clinging to old traditional values, the DPP is aggressively looking between ideals and reality for solutions.

As long as an issue benefits all the people no subject is beyond the DPP's concern. This is why the DPP is not just a party that resolves old problems, but one that raises new issues to the forefront.

In the composition of our administrative team, we do not advocate bringing all of society's best and brightest into the political arena, but rather insist that opportunities for political involvement be expanded into the private arena so as to bring about true partnership between government and the private sector. This is why the new DPP will not create closed cliques, but actively expand open political networks.

The new DPP on the road to taking power calls for a new definition of the Democratic Progressive Party: that is, the DPP is no longer just an opposition party counter to the Kuomintang, and no longer just a party supported by people born in Taiwan, but a new political party leading all of Taiwan into the 21st century and advancing Taiwan's ascension on the world stage.

Chapter Six

Phase Two Reform

Taiwan has given us hope, just as she has let us down. But we can never allow ourselves to become despondent. We have given the Kuomintang plenty of chances, but they have always relied on local factions to maintain power, are feeble when it comes to handling black-gold politics, and always resort to appealing for stability to disguise their own ineptitude. This is why Taiwan's second phase of reform must look to the Democratic Progressive Party to assume executive power. The alternation of political parties will assure the eradication of the roots of the mafia-and-money black-gold alliance, injecting new blood into "shareholders' Taiwan." With these changes, a young Taiwan is right around the corner.

Establishing a tri-power presidential system

Reform is never easy. In his political classic, The Prince, 16th century Italian Nicolo Machiavelli wrote:

> And it ought to be remembered that there is nothing more difficult to take in hand, more perilous to conduct, or more uncertain in its success, than to take the lead in the introduction of a new order of things. Because the innovator has for enemies all those who have done well under the old conditions, and lukewarm defenders in those who may do well under the new. This coolness arises partly from fear of the opponents, who have the laws on their side, and partly from the incredulity of men, who do not readily believe in new things until they have had a long experience of them.

The resistance of conservative forces, and the incredulity of the majority, often strikes fear in reformers about the risks involved, causing them to lose their drive to reform. This is akin to compromising with the forces of the old order. No one will deny the democratic reforms promoted by President Lee Teng-hui since 1988, but since becoming the first popularly elected president of Taiwan in 1996, Lee Teng-hui's reforms have lost momentum. Before 1996 a struggle was underway between reform and anti-reform, and the respective "mainstream" and "non-mainstream" factions of the KMT. However, once Lee Teng-hui gained a firm grasp on the reins of state power, all reform has targeted the KMT interest group. Not only has this halted the pace of reform, it has even spurred the consolidation of the entire interest group, dashing the people's hopes in Lee Teng-hui for reform.

This is why Taiwan must enter the second phase of political reform, and only via alternating party rule can phase two reforms build abounding momentum for progress!

In the 11 years that Lee Teng-hui has administered the government, the National Assembly has amended the constitution five times. In recent years, nearly every year there have been calls for further modifications, yet each modification arouses popular disgust. Multiple constitutional revisions have bankrupted the National Assembly's credibility, and undermined the stability of the constitutional framework. Why, with each revision, has the constitution of the Republic of China become increasingly jumbled, at the same time losing the people's trust?

The crux of the problem is the contradictory nature of the constitution itself. Looking back at history, when the Kuomintang government in Nanjing wrote the constitution, the civil war between the Nationalists and Communist Party was still raging. The communists boycotted the formulation of the constitution, Chiang Kai-shek lost authority, and the Political Consultative Conference became an arena of intra-party struggle. Zhang Junli, writer of the constitutional draft, advocated a cabinet system of administration, while Chiang Kai-shek favored a presidential arrangement. Following all sorts of wheeling and dealing, bargaining, and compromise, the various factions formulated the Republic of China Constitution, a document that fails to delineate either a cabinet- or presidential-based government structure.

After retreating to Taiwan, Chiang Kai-shek and his son, Chiang Ching-kuo, suspended the constitution and ruled under marshal law justified by Temporary Provisions Effective During the Period of Communist Rebellion (or the "Provisional Articles of the Constitution"). Thus, under the Chiangs' rule, Taiwan never enjoyed even a day of constitutional government. Then, when President Lee Teng-hui took power and sought to implement a democratic constitutional government, society finally realized that the ROC Constitution is riddled with contradictions hampering implementation. And while President Lee Teng-hui's friction with successive premiers Lee Huan and Hao Bei-tsun were rooted in conflicts between the mainstream and non-mainstream factions, and the forces of reform and anti-reform, they can also be partly attributed to the structural contradictions of the constitution.

While all quarters were intent on making alterations to the ROC Constitution, accommodating a contradiction-filled constitution is like repairing an automobile: no matter how much work is done on an old jalopy, it can never be turned into a new model. Meanwhile, factoring in Lee Teng-hui's constant reconciliation with political reality, each new constitutional modification has carried with it a host of other consequences.

The constitution, inconsequential in the eyes of the martial law rulers, bears absolute consequence in a democratic nation. The constitution is both an outline for national governance and the symbol of the safeguarding of the public's rights. At the same time, the constitution is the highest law, conferring powers while limiting them at the same time. The constitution is a government's operative tool, and a constraining force on the government.

Tocqueville's "Democracy in America" has given me tremendous inspiration. Tocqueville believed that a new political philosophy is necessary to establish a new political order, and that this new philosophy must be founded upon the basic principle of popular sovereignty. The classic example of this philosophy is the Constitution of the United States of America. The US Constitution benefits from the spirit of "separation of powers" and "checks and balances, and the local autonomy instituted since the 17th and 18th centuries. In today's Taiwan, if we are to put an end to the haphazard modification of the constitution by the National Assembly and establish a stable constitution, we must learn from the democratic spirit of the United States Constitution.

In 1787, the Constitutional Convention was held in Philadelphia, ostensibly to establish a strong federal government. However, the framers of the U.S. Constitution met to debate two crucial considerations: First, the powers of the federal government and local governments must be clearly delineated. Second, executive, legislative, and judicial powers should be separated in such a way as to allow for checks and balances. Their framework works like this: The president can veto laws formulated by the congress. Similarly, even laws passed by congress and signed by the president can be declared null by the Supreme Court if deemed unconstitutional. Meanwhile, the president, with the approval of the Senate, can make appointments to the

Supreme Court to oversee the execution of the law. The congress controls budgetary matters, and the House of Representatives and the Senate, the two bodies that compose the congress, have veto power over one another, and bills must have the approval of both houses before becoming laws. This, in essence, is checks and balances, and parity of powers and responsibilities, in action. It has also served as the basis for the stable United States political structure for over 200 years.

In contrast, under the current constitutional structure of the Republic of China, the president is barely subject to the scrutiny of congress, giving him power without attendant responsibility; meanwhile, the premier has responsibility without substantive power. Moreover, the Kuomintang clings to a five-power constitution and five-yuan (body) structure. An oddity among the systems of the world's democratic nations, it effectively prevents the separation and balance of powers.

Given the current political situation in Taiwan, further modifications made under the framework of the existing ROC Constitution will only create more disorder and fragmentation. Consequently, it is incumbent upon the second popularly elected president of the ROC to convene a constitutional reform convention, enlisting political party delegates, respected authorities, and experts in constitutional law to engage in debate, reach consensus and move toward adoption of a structure characterized by separation of executive, judicial, and legislative powers. This will be one of the key political undertakings of Phase Two Political Reform.

The end of black-gold politics and the alternation of political party power

The grave state of black-gold politics has been noted by Dr. Lee Yuan-tseh, president of Academia Sinica, who lamented that over one-half of Taiwan's local people's representatives are connected with the underworld of organized crime. Despite Taiwan's democratization, the rule of law has yet to be truly implemented, in part due to the workings of black-gold politics. This unholy alliance between government, big money, and organized crime goes beyond the corruption of political mores —economically, it creates an unfair competitive environment; socially, it has led to the tragic shooting of an innocent pregnant woman shopping in a department store. Like everyone else, I have a family, a wife, and children. Each time I see the carefree smile of a young child and think of the worsening environment in which they live today, I feel a knot in my chest.

For these reasons, the second main theme of Phase Two Political Reforms is "the end of Black-Gold influence over government." To thoroughly resolve the influence of organized crime and big money over normal government operation, we must first familiarize ourselves with the factors that have led to this alliance.

The black-gold problem did not begin yesterday; rather, it is the result of historical circumstances. **For the past half century, the Kuomintang has relied extensively on alliances with local factions**

to prop up its rule. In turn, the deep frictions among local factions are the result of long-term division and indulgence by the KMT. However, the lifting of marshal law[13] was like opening Pandora's Box. Lacking the constraints of a clearly delineated legal framework, Taiwan has seen the rapid deterioration of public safety, the alliance of local factions and organized crime, and the deepening of the KMT's ties with organized crime and big money. These factors, **combined with the catalytic affect of the KMT's party-run enterprises, have made black-gold politics the norm in Taiwanese society today.**

Under popular scrutiny in recent years, government authorities have started to become alert to the seriousness of black-gold politics. Nevertheless, as the maintenance of power continues to claim top priority, the ruling authorities fold their arms and allow underworld big wigs to become bullies in the Legislative Yuan, and kleptocrats to become members of congress. Frequent tales circulate describing how organized crime runs amok in villages and neighborhoods, while collusion between government and business, running deeper yet, is even more immune to reform. This situation has amply proven that if we continue to give the KMT an open-ended ticket to governing

---

[13] Marshal law was first declared in Taiwan when Chiang Kai-shek sent his troops to Taiwan to quell a popular backlash against the KMT regime now known as the February 28 Incident, in which as many as 20,000 lives were lost. Once public order had been re-established by the KMT, marshal law was temporarily lifted, only to be reinstated again on 19 May 1949. Under martial law, myriad laws, regulations, and executive orders deprived Taiwanese their basic human rights, and "Provisional Articles of the Constitution" (also known by the full name Temporary Provisions in Effect During the Period of Communist Rebellion) replaced the original ROC Constitution. After over 38 years in effect, the longest of any nation in the modern era, marshal law was finally lifted on 15 July 1987.

Taiwan, black-gold troubles will only worsen.

We can no longer look to the KMT to resolve black-gold issues on its own volition, just as we cannot expect a person to cut off his right hand with his left. The KMT's default on one of the points of consensus of the National Development Conference[14] , the suspension of future elections at the village and district levels, is the clearest example. The KMT and the mafia-money structure are Siamese twins —joined at the hip —thus it follows that the KMT is unable to resolve this situation on its own.

Although the Taiwanese people have exhibited courage and spurned the mafia-money structure, the public must continue to demonstrate the wisdom to bring about a cleansing of politics, fair competition, and a secure society, all of which can be accomplished via the alternate assumption of power by various political parties.

Judging by the performance of DPP administrative chiefs in cities and counties throughout Taiwan, the majority vouches for the DPP's characteristic clean and efficient administrative style. In the future, having gained executive control over the central government, **the DPP shall attack the scourge of black-gold politics as a systemic problem, taking concrete, progressive, and pragmatic steps towards a thorough solution.**

---

[14] During the summer of 1996, President Lee Teng-hui convened a National Development Conference to gather consensus for constitutional modifications. In turn for DPP support of the conference's resolutions, the ruling KMT pledged to institute a number of reforms, including the termination of elections for village- and district-level representatives.

Following broad consultation with others and thorough rumination, I propose the following eight concrete reform measures:

1. A special prosecutor, appointed by the president, will conduct a full-scale investigation into vote buying, prosecuting where sufficient evidence warrants such action.

2. The president shall appoint the director of the Bureau of Investigation to conduct surveillance and gather evidence on Taiwan's main criminal organizations and political figures with backgrounds in organized crime, prosecuting where evidence warrants such action.

3. Revision of legal statutes, so that individuals with prior criminal records related to organized crime may not run for any form of public office.

4. Implementation of one of the points of consensus reached during the National Development Conference: suspension of all further village and district-level elections, to sever the closely-knit ties between organized crime and local factions.

5. Promote the institution of a small election district system, such as practiced in the United States and Japan, in which candidates are nominated by political parties to thoroughly eliminate vote buying.

6. Establish a non-partisan independent financial investigation committee to conduct a full examination of Taiwan's financial institutions and serve as a watchdog to forestall financial crime and government-business collusion.

7. Via amendment of the constitution or relevant legal codes, demand that political parties may not operate businesses. After assuming

executive power, the Democratic Progressive Party, following the letter of the law and adhering to principles of fairness and justice, will undertake a general inventory of all KMT party-run businesses, returning money that belongs to the people.

8. Establish a "Justice Reform Supervisory Committee" composed of members of the legal profession, public sector, and academic community to draft a timetable and supervise the successive institution of various legal reforms.

For these concrete steps to become tangible political momentum, the DPP must take over from the KMT as Taiwan's ruling party. In practice, this means that only by allowing political parties to move in and out of power, so that the ruling party implements clean, efficient government, while the minority party serves as an effective opposition party, can Taiwan shake off the nightmare of mafia-money politics forever and become a civilized nation rooted in democracy and the rule of law. As the only candidate with absolutely zero ties to the KMT, I am the only one who can stand as one with the people once elected, to safeguard our way of life and the happy smiles on our children's faces.

A new political approach: assuming a stake in Taiwan

In addition to the second phase of political reforms, I believe that Taiwan must engage in a "conceptual revolution." Taiwanese in the new century will manifest the following understanding: **power shall not exist without corresponding accountability; public authority**

shall not come without democracy; freedom means self-regulation, diversification, and concern for social justice.

Assuming risks and securing the future, central tenets gleaned from UK Prime Minister Tony Blair's writings, illuminate the way toward deepening these concepts.

Tony Blair believes that each citizen is inextricably linked with England's national interests. Under this ideal, Blair wants every individual to have a job, skills, a family, opportunities, and responsibilities. This way, every citizen shall yield dividends from a prosperous and stable England, forming a unit of shared destiny where honor and interests are shared by all.

Over the course of more than a decade of tremendous transition, Taiwan has begun to progress toward nation building. However, on a societal level, to truly become an advanced nation, Taiwan must further promote the second phase of reforms. **With the unique characteristics of Taiwanese society in mind, I propose the new concept of "assuming a stake in Taiwan" in the hope that we invest in a new Taiwan together:**

1. The political concept of "assuming a stake in Taiwan" emphasizes an open, trusting, confident attitude towards allowing the people to develop their full potential and asking that citizens boldly take responsibility. Over the course of this process, the government plays an advisory role in elevating individual potential and promoting fairness in society. In the service of these objectives, the government must regenerate into a young, energetic organization, transforming

from an autocratic government into a civil, democratic government. As citizens enjoy certain rights and privileges, the government should exemplify the spirit of political accountability.

Only when the government takes the initiative to innovate, transform, and give the people a sense of involvement can a "shareholder" consciousness take shape and partnerships form between central and local governments, and between the government and the people. The central government should relinquish authority to enable local government greater autonomy. Central government and local government powers and rational budget allocation should be clearly delineated on constitutional and legislative levels. This way, given the opportunity to take part in the regeneration of government organizations, the people will establish personal relations as "shareholders" in the new government.

2. **The economic concept of "assuming a stake in Taiwan" emphasizes partnership between government and enterprise. With this partnership, the government becomes a promoter rather than a ruler, and appeals to public interest in place of engaging in ideological struggle.** Government authorities need not engage in the direct operation of enterprises, but must concentrate on tangible efforts to promote the following fiscal policies: 1) provide a low-interest environment that promotes long-term investment; 2) secure highly qualified personnel for business and industry through education; 3) provide high quality infrastructure works; 4) joint promotion of local and small- to medium-sized business development by the government and the business community; 5) provide an export-oriented commercial environment;

6) forge a potent yet harmonious labor-capital environment to resolve unemployment and social welfare issues.

The above six points are all main components in the fiscal policy of modern nations. Government must devote efforts to revitalizing the economy and creating employment opportunities. Therefore, the government should focus on the following main objectives: Full promotion of educational reform and scientific research; appropriation of ample budgetary resources for transportation and infrastructure development, and development of an island-wide public transportation network; improvement of the tax structure to stimulate venture capital investment; formulation of financial and monetary policy in line with actual needs.

3. **The social concept of "assuming a stake in Taiwan" emphasizes the establishment of community awareness, founded upon core values such as the establishment of social groups, fairness and equality, common goals, and collective assumption of responsibilities.**

In the wake of the 21 September 1999 earthquake, one could sense a shift in the value system of the Taiwanese people, from "self-interest" toward "group interest," from the "me" generation toward the "we" generation. The young, vigorous new 21st century Taiwanese government should work toward deepening and implementing of the following social concepts: 1) Ensure the right to survival, so that everyone can have a job; 2) ensure everyone has the chance to improve their own life through equal access to education; 3) encourage everyone to foster community consciousness. With these goals in mind, the government should propose concrete public policy measures concerning employment, housing mortgages, education, community, and public safety, forming partnerships between the government, individuals, and communities.

How should we go about implementing the new concept of "assuming a stake in Taiwan?" We can use US President Bill Clinton as an example, who discovered that the people are highly concerned with such "value issues" as social welfare, the budget deficit, environment, and crime rates. In response, he highlighted these value issues and enlisted scholars and experts to draft a set of public policies, using the presidential campaign to ignite debate on these issues and thereby activating public involvement.

In addition, President Clinton often takes cabinet members, members of congress, and mavericks of industry deep into economically backward areas on "journeys of opportunity." Clinton's motivation is crystal clear: to highlight local needs through "journeys of opportunity," thereby introducing infrastructure development, private investment, and vocational education to drive economic growth in backward areas.

Clinton's "journeys of opportunity" help forge "shareholder relationships" among government, businesses, and communities. In particular, promotion of infrastructure development, private investment, and vocational training helps foster community autonomy and a sense of involvement. I believe that government should work closely with community reformers, offering small loans to community members or disadvantaged groups to start businesses, and offer tax reduction incentives to attract private enterprise to invest in development of relatively backward areas. These are examples of where "assuming a stake in Taiwan" must be nurtured.

Based on the above understanding, the new phase of reforms must accommodate the trend toward democratic constitutional government, so that constitutional reform, in line with Taiwan's unique requirements, transcends pointless debates on the merits of presidential or cabinet systems and progresses towards a three-power presidential structure. I am sure the road will not be easy, but the second popularly elected president, as someone genuinely concerned with Taiwan's future, must have the intestinal fortitude to advance major political projects that determine the release of Taiwan's vitality.

At the same time, on the occasion of the millennial presidential election, I appeal to voters to vote the DPP into the central government and open a new page of alternating political power. By allowing power to change hands back and forth between political parties at all levels of government, we can undermine the black-gold power structure and put the legacy of this unholy alliance forever in the past. Further, the concept of "assuming a stake in Taiwan" can help foster a deeper sense of autonomy among the people, thereby stimulating active involvement and carrying Taiwan forward into a new era. The accomplishment of these objectives will bring Taiwan's true vitality into the spotlight, becoming a guarantee of success in the new century.

Chapter Seven

New 21st Century Leadership

*T*he breadth of the hearts and minds of 21st century *leaders is the key to new leadership. Choosing the right people for the right jobs, striking a balance between two extremes, a keen grasp of consensus in society... these point the course for Taiwan's development. I am prepared to propose my vision and objectives, to share them with the people, communicate candidly, and build confidence in order that a borderless government organization can guide Taiwan's transformation into a learning society. These are my basic motivations for my New Middle Road. I am sure that Taiwan's future leaders will all exhibit similar vision and breadth of mind.*

The four components of new leadership

The new century beckons. Society in the 21st century shall be dominated by two kinds of people, "know-how" people and "organizational" people. "Know-how" people possess general decision-making abilities, and are capable of utilizing organization to resolve various problems. "Organizational" types are in the habit of dividing tasks to get maximum results out of know-how through teamwork. As Taiwan enters the 21st century, we need to form a new leadership team out of know-how and organizational people who possess a global perspective, local consciousness, rigorous analytical skills, and a fine cultural and humanistic sensitivity. This new team will be equipped to take Taiwan into the ranks of the world's developed countries.

I am reminded of a medieval European allegory that goes like this: A man was walking down the street when he spotted a stone mason at work. He asked the mason, "What are you up to?" to which the mason replied, "I'm chipping stone." At the next corner, the man came across another mason and asked him the same question. This time the mason answered, " I'm carving a pillar." At the next corner, encountering yet another mason at work, he asked the same question again. This stone mason answered, "I'm building a grand cathedral."

The first two stone masons knew only to grit their teeth and throw themselves into their work, naturally fulfilling their obligations. However, a grand cathedral cannot be constructed without the third stone mason, for he sees beyond the task at hand to the whole picture and grand vision.

To me, this is a quality that every fine leader must possess. After all, **the 21st century is the age of globalization —a society of know-how and organizational people.** Any 21st century leader must be able to respond to the needs of the era, be capable of self-transformation and betterment, and possess a broad overall perspective.

The new leadership of the 21st century must tap into the "intellectual capital" of the people, inspiring popular confidence and mobilizing the people's potential and ideals so that followers become leaders' partners, boosting the power of reform.

During my term as mayor of Taipei, and as since leaving office, I have always made the forging of new leadership one of the main aspects of my thinking. I believe that this new leadership force is created with the combination of the following four key components:

1. **New leadership must propose a vision and objectives.** As with the allegory related above, new leadership is not about chipping stones or carving pillars, but constructing grand cathedrals. Leaders must continually ask themselves: "What are the objectives of my work? How should I proceed toward those objectives?"

Taking Taiwan for example, cross-strait relations and national security are sensitive issues that concern everybody. Everybody wants to see Taiwan and China establish peaceful dialogue and exchange, yet we must also be able to resist the use of military force by China against Taiwan. At the same time, we want to play a part in the international community, particularly maintaining sturdy friendships and defensive relations with the United States and Japan. Responding to the people's collective needs, a leader must provide a clear, tangible, yet viable vision for Taiwan's diplomacy and cross-strait relations. This vision, in turn, must comply with the collective consciousness and values of Taiwanese society for the given leader to deserve credibility.

Over the past several years I have presented my views on such issues as national security and cross-strait relations on many occasions in the effort to gain popular appreciation and support of a viable vision.

2. **New leadership must engage in frank communication with the people.** Communication is not a one-way process of "me" to "you"; rather, it involves two-way exchange between "us." Communication is human power, and like a car's engine, requires regular maintenance. Like everything else, without regular maintenance, interpersonal relationships become rusty.

Take for example finance and economics, an issue that concerns everybody. How can the economy be stimulated? How can the employment rate be raised? And what tangible policies do leaders proffer? These questions must be discussed via frank, two-way communication between leaders and the people. New leadership means listening to what the people are saying; it means accountability, open-mindedness, explaining things in detail to the people in a candid manner, and using communication to establish shared ideas and resolve. A leader who communicates frankly, who speaks rationally with the people, is the only kind of leader capable of transforming a political culture of friction.

3. New leadership can foster popular confidence. Taiwanese incomes have long been in the same league as the citizens of the advanced nations of the West, yet their quality of life and their living environment compares to that of most developing nations. As mayor of Taipei, I approached efforts towards raising the quality of life and the environment in Taipei from the perspective of a "municipal manager." These efforts attracted the notice of authorities around the world, who selected Taipei as one of Asia's best cities, serving to show that as long as we are confident there is nothing we can't change.

With this in mind, new leadership means proposing "rights of the living," coming up with concrete solutions in areas including public safety, transportation, air pollution, environmental protection, ecological preservation, and national land planning. Rooted in thorough understanding of the people's concerns, these solutions can rebuild the public's confidence and dignity through improvement of the quality of life. In this way, the people will identify with the land upon which they live, getting to know Taiwan as **The New Taiwanese Family,** identifying with Taiwan, and "managing" Taiwan together.

4. New leadership can build a society that continues to enhance knowledge throughout a lifetime. The 21st century will be an age characterized by human compassion, cultural and artistic renaissance, religious revival, community awareness, rational thinking, and volunteerism. In this age, leaders must act as "educators" to drive a lifelong learning movement, working to foster "intelligent organizations" and a society of citizens oriented towards a lifetime of learning.

As the philosopher Baruch (Benedict) Spinoza said, the highest state of human activity is learning. Learning means understanding, and as long as this understanding goes deep enough we can avoid making the same mistakes over again. Taiwanese leaders of the next century must treat educational reform and scientific research as Taiwan's greatest "intellectual capital." **My concept of a "know-how Taiwan" aims to work with citizens to establish a society of people who never stop learning throughout their lives.**

To survive in an environment of intense global competition, Taiwan must be equipped with a "global operational approach," approaching the training of leaders with an eye towards global competitiveness and a broad international perspective. Michael E. Porter of the Harvard Business School has advanced the concept of "the competitive advantage of nations." Porter believes that enterprises must create added value, formulate brand-new business strategies, thoroughly revamp organizational structure, enhance personnel training, set strict demands for quality and assimilate new talents and forward-looking concepts. These are the chief objectives of the new leadership I seek.

Human resources: the cornerstone of national administration

During the quiet period I spent reflecting and studying after leaving office as mayor of Taipei, I read the autobiography of Tokugawa Iemitsu （德川家康） very closely. As a young man, Tokugawa Iemitsu began to see himself in an abstract way, not as a "natural man" but as a "legal entity." This approach allowed him to jump outside the confines of ego and see the world in an objective manner. He took this approach to jude the veracity of things, listen to opinions from all sides, and only then propose a response. He treated and managed himself as an "object" as opposed to the subject, enabling him to resolve issues thanks to his tremendous restraint, sensibility, and self-control.

In addition to this personality trait, Tokugawa Iemitsu's success had a great deal to do with his brain trust (management team). In other words, human resources are the cornerstone of national administration, and a capacity to surround himself with talented people of diverse capabilities enabled Tokugawa Iemitsu, starting with nothing, to go so far.

Tokugawa Iemitsu created an environment of free discussion, allowing members of his brain trust to express their opinions without reserve. Through constructive debate, ample digestion, absorption of intelligence, and criticism from opposing viewpoints, together they ensured the appropriateness of their decision-making. Their example illustrates the fact that decision-making cannot rely strictly on "experience," but also takes "debate" in order to capture the essence of a given problem. By creating a forum for interaction among these talented individuals, Tokugawa Iemitsu was able to perceive the essence of politics and formulate appropriate measures in response.

Tokugawa Iemitsu said, "I do not possess any particular gifts, but I believe that when I face the moment of truth, the loyal people who are willing to sacrifice their lives for me will be my most treasured gifts." With this quote, Tokugawa Iemitsu encapsulates the importance of human resources. Talented people must be regarded as public assets, as opposed to tools, and leaders must know how best to recognize and place the right people in the right positions to make great things happen. In the "On Governing" chapter of his Analects, the sage Confucius himself echoed this concept, saying: "If you govern with the power of your virtue, you will be like the North Star. It just stays in its place while all the other stars position themselves around it." Naturally, this is the highest yardstick by which a leader can be measured.

Among modern states, Singapore's elder statesman, Lee Kwan Yew, is one man who treats people as the cornerstone of state administration and has incorporated that tenet into his administrative system. Lee's methods for training people merit close attention. I have sought wisdom from Lee Kwan Yew on many occasions. His political concerns have always centered on a single theme: how to establish a good government. To establish a good government, it is necessary to recruit top caliber people to manage the government. To wit, Lee has said: "I feel that the most sobering political problem Singapore faces today is how do we get young people willing to take the baton from us within the next decade?"

Lee Kwan Yew has posited the so-called "helicopter quality" as a key to leadership strength. By this, Lee means that leaders must be able to see far and wide as from a helicopter, at the same time they must be able to plant their feet firmly on the ground, working diligently like a helicopter taking off and landing. A helicopter-like leader must possess three key capacities: 1) analytical ability; 2) a reasonable grasp of the facts; 3) close investigation of significant details and pursuit of principles.

Lee Kwan Yew built a talent pool of 200 candidates for Singapore's ruling People's Action Party (PAP), attracting talent to official government positions with generous compensation, much like a corporation. We might have differences of opinion with Lee over his interpretation of "Asian style democracy," but when it comes to cultivating talent Lee Kwan Yew deserves a closer look.

As a legislator cultivating my congressional staff, and later putting together my Taipei City Hall administrative team, I have always known that the complexity of modern politics and the breadth of specialization that it demands, cannot rely on individualistic political stars; rather, one must enlist the assistance of professionals working according to their strengths. As mayor, I chose people for their abilities, regardless of party affiliation, family or ethnic background, or sex. This held true for men, and just as equally for women, because I have always believed that **people comprise our most important resource.**

Personnel demands constant thought. For instance, how can we cultivate people to run the country amidst international competition?

How can we redefine the aims, values, and substance of education? How can we foster motivated and responsible people, and turn know-how into productivity and competitiveness? And how can we employ government resources to assist the private sector to establish channels to attract qualified people?

The new leadership force of the 21st century means using people to conduct "adaptation leadership," engendering changes in values through leadership. All leaders must have an open heart and mind, soak up information, embrace a broad range of people, and establish their own core brain trust. Only in such a way can they mobilize the energy of their people, encouraging followers to constantly progress into members of the leadership group themselves, and ensuring that leadership becomes a force equipped to promote the second phase of reforms and shape Taiwan into a new enlightened society.

The ultimate concerns of the president

Leaders and managers are not one in the same. Leaders "do the right thing," including presenting their vision, goals, and issues, establishing a model of words and actions with which they affect their followers. Meanwhile, managers "do it right,' including completion, responsibility for, handling, and execution of various affairs. Leaders think strategically and philosophically; meanwhile, managers think tactically, aiming for efficiency.

Other than the powers conferred by the constitution, the president must fulfill the following functions in the capacity as the nation's leader: 1. Raise issues and formulate strategy, to attract popular support and attention. 2. Propose a vision and goals. 3. Through words and actions, set a model for others, assuring the public's confidence and hopes. 4. Possess the mettle to take responsibility; have excellent communication skills, so as to build credibility for the administration. 5. Put together an efficient management team; apply collective will and strength.

In order to put these functions to work, I believe that **"speed, simplicity, and confidence" encapsulate the decision-making qualities of Taiwan's future president.**

"Speed, simplicity, and confidence" is a new management approach, action philosophy, and new leadership force. The leading exponent of this approach is none other than Jack Welch, CEO of General Electric. Welch believes that in the future, organizations will be without tangible limitations, and that people will engage in communication and discussion in an open, unrestricted environment. Under this environment, people will absorb information at maximum speed, responding rapidly in turn, breaking down internal and external walls and hierarchy. Having accomplished this, they apply their "intellectual capital" to achieve high productivity.

Working within a borderless organization, leaders must keep everything simple, using the simplest concepts and language to communicate, because simple, straightforward, candid, sincere communication is infectious, and can inspire people's passion for work, fill them with energy, and make them willing to devote themselves to an ideal. When a leader possesses the individual qualities of speed and simplicity, his confidence becomes the source and inspiration for group confidence.

The success of "dynamic management" in our New City Hall Movement demonstrates that an organization can and should be full of energy and flexibility. I gained precious insight from Welch's concept of the borderless organization: the top priorities for any leader include seeking, valuing, and cultivating the opinions and self-esteem of every person, on all fronts, for this is the key to success as a leader.

Leaders place the right people in the right positions, and spend money in the most appropriate places to achieve optimal distribution. In a word, leaders are people who accurately convey ideas and correctly allocate resources. A leader is a good coach, who creates an atmosphere of learning, values intellectual resources, steers group synergy, and establishes competitive advantage.

Modern society is global and information-oriented. We must rapidly absorb and digest new knowledge, and drawing on ample human sensitivity, make rapid and correct decisions.

For the presidential campaign, I have proposed the themes "young Taiwan, energetic government" in the hope that the government of the future will be a "borderless organization" with the efficiency of a corporate organization, to become an engine driving society's constant progress.

Confronted by the challenges of forbidding conditions at home and abroad, the president must embody the qualities detailed below, all of which I seek to fulfill through constant self-transformation and self-improvement: 1. Capable of handling crises; exhibits moral fortitude, rational thought, and determination. 2. Knows how to find and use talent, regardless of ethnic background or party affiliation. 3. Is a leader for spiritual development, as well as the strongest, most enduring emotional core for the collective. 4. Capable of determining administrative priorities; possesses a keen sensitivity toward national security, financial policy, and public policy, and the ability to articulate viewpoints on these issues. 5. Communicates effectively, and is able to communicate with the people as well as opponents. 6. An efficient administrative manager, capable of organizing efficient teams to institute policy.

Possessing the above-mentioned personality characteristics, **Taiwan's president must appreciate** the importance of "the will to survive": domestically, this means forging a secure environment founded upon the rule of law, to allow the Taiwanese people to find the meaning in living and appreciate the dignity of life. Externally, it requires the confidence necessary to resist the threat of foreign force. As Nietzsche said, The strong will of life is a bright lantern for the world." Over the history of human civilization, technological backslides and outside encroachment have never been the main contributors to civilization's decline, but if people lose the will to survive, civilization is thrown into ruin.

Taiwan has always possessed tremendous vitality, the driving force behind the progressive march to today's accomplishments. But when confronting the complex environment of globalization the future holds in store, relying on the discretional advancement of the people is unreliable; rather, we need a new leader with a broad vision, capable of making decisions and spurring the people's vast energies to forge a "young Taiwan."

Over the course of constant challenges from inside and out, the president is bound by the responsibility and obligation to translate external challenges into internal motivation, to delineate a vision for a new Taiwanese society, and set the stage for the regeneration of Taiwan.

On many occasions since becoming involved in politics, I have had the chance to listed to others speak their minds, expressing their hopes and desires. In general, the people are most concerned with their immediate lives and their futures. They want security and development in their current lives, and a future to look forward to and to achieve. The collective consciousness we share is the map that guides us forward together.

I once listened to a scholar introduce the work of the father of psychoanalysis, Sigmund Freud. The most intriguing aspect to me was Freud's expectations for the progress of humanity. He believed that humanity's progress must take four paths simultaneously:1. Anything having to do with the transformation of nature by human beings belongs to the realm of civilization; 2. Other hallmarks of civilization are beauty, cleanliness, and order; 3. Humanity's noble spiritual activities belong to the realm of civilization as well, and religious faith and philosophical thought have the power to lead humans to a higher state; harmonization of human relations is an emblem of civilization.

I long to reach these markers of civilization together with the Taiwanese people, for we should turn Taiwanese culture into a harmonious, shared civilization, boasting a fine quality of life and an enlightening impact on humanity. People and other people, people and the environment, and Taiwan and the world at large, are like a series of flawless concentric circles packed with energy, stable and in equilibrium, extending outward. **Starting with "what we have," we determine "what we want to be," and then we arrive there.**

We will be strong children of Taiwan, vigorous and determined. Taiwan is our home, and will one day become a jewel in the sea envied around the world.

A president must become a lighthouse guiding the way. I'm prepared to be just that.

The 21st century will surely be a century full of challenges. Confronting the challenges of the new century, cultivating new leadership is a sure way for Taiwan to enhance her chances of survival. This new leadership force must inspire people, so that high caliber people can maximize their contribution in the right places. Only in this way can we employ our abundant talent pool in the new century to shape Taiwan's future. As talent requires constant cultivation and patronage, turning to factions, ethnic groups, or sex to pick and choose people will only dig our own graves. Lastly, **the core of the leadership is the president. Thus the president must have an ultimate concern, so that under the president's direction all leaders and managers can assume responsibility for taking Taiwan into the future,** and while striving towards this ultimate concern, map out a shared vision for all Taiwanese.

This is power, and now this power has direction.

Chapter Eight

Establishing a New Taiwanese Family

Body after cold body. Perhaps we crossed paths before, or perhaps not. The devastating September 21 earthquake threw our compatriots, in whom the same blood flows, into a living hell. This scene not only rocked the souls of the Taiwanese, but it stirred their power. Volunteers from around the country, working as one in the rescue effort, not only restored confidence in themselves, while restoring the faith of others, but they also re-established faith in the land. Witnessing the power of rebirth during the restoration effort has been like a second baptism of my soul. And throughout this difficult process, we have seen a glimpse of the vision of a "volunteer Taiwan" that I proposed earlier.

The fresh vision of a "Volunteer Taiwan"

The Chichi earthquake that struck on 21 September 1999 is now a part of the historical memory of the Taiwanese people. Over more than a century, the shared historical memory of the Taiwanese has been largely political, and mostly connected to oppression by outside forces. Such historical events as the 1895 Treaty of Shimonoseki[15] and the February 28th Incident of 1947[16] , make up part of the historical memory of our grandfathers and our fathers; the Kaohsiung Incident of 1979, meanwhile, is an unforgettable case of political persecution for our own generation.

Compared to such political incidents, however, the September 21 earthquake was more devastating yet, its consequences longer lasting,

---

[15] Entered between China and Japan on April 17, 1895, ending the First Sino-Japanese War 1884-85), the Treaty of Shimonoseki was negotiated and signed by Ito Hirobumi for Japan and Li Hongzhang for China. Taking advantage of China's spectacular defeat, Japan imposed harsh terms on China. The treaty provided for the end of Chinese suzerainty over Korea, giving Korea independence, and for the cession to Japan in perpetuity of Taiwan, the Pescadores (Penghu) islands, plus Port Arthur and the Liaodong peninsula. Japan also imposed a large indemnity and forced China to open five new treaty ports. However, just a week after the treaty was signed, Russia, France, and Germany together demanded that Japan renounce claims to Port Arthur and the Liaodong Peninsula. Japan reluctantly agreed (Nov. 1895), but China was forced to pay an additional indemnity, adding salt to her wounds in a series of events considered the final great humiliation in China's imperial history.

[16] Despite its name, the February 28th Incident was an extended crackdown by the Kuomintang on local dissent in Taiwan. See footnote in Chapter Six for a fuller description.

and its impact on the hearts and minds of the Taiwanese people indelible. If something good has come from this disaster, it is that a "new Taiwanese family" —together for better or worse, in life and death —has arisen. **Before the September 21 earthquake Taiwan lived in a "me" era,** but ever since the earthquake it has become a new "us" era, and with its arrival Taiwan has moved from a "self-interest" orientation in a new "collective interest" direction. It is in such an era that "volunteer Taiwan" can make a difference.

Before I go into detail explaining my concept of "volunteer Taiwan," I would like to talk about two thinkers who have influenced me. The first is American sociological thinker Francis Fukuyama, and the other is U.S. management guru Peter Drucker.

In the midst of the Labour Party transformation, British Prime Minister Tony Blair said that Labour is not just the party of an individual, but that of the community. In his writings, Blair refers repeatedly to Fukuyama's concept of "trust." According to Fukuyama's analysis, any country looking to stand out in the 21st century must meet three conditions: democratic politics, a market economy, and a civil society. A young, energetic civil society is the only way to build a stable political and economic structure. In other words, in addition to such "institutional" regulators as laws, contracts, and economic rationality, such intangibles as caring and trust, moral obligation, and social responsibility in human interaction are equally vital. Trust is "social capital" that determines whether a civilized country can continue to progress. Giving examples from the development of democratic politics and economics in the United States, Germany, and Japan, Fukuyama explains how "trust" is actually the most important indicator of progress.

A philosopher of another sort who merits our attention is business management guru Peter Drucker, who calls on the leaders of the world's nations in the 21st century to pay attention to two issues. First, governments must regain control over domestic economic and fiscal policy, no longer taking a laissez-faire approach, in order to keep budget deficits from spiraling out of control and leading to national bankruptcy. Second, governments must cease and realign traditional "welfare state" policies, as governments should work together with the volunteer force of business and the private sector to resolve issues of social welfare. Drucker's ideas have long attracted the attention of global leaders, among them U.S. President Bill Clinton and British Prime Minister Tony Blair, who made balancing their countries' respective budgets key platform issues, winning popular support. Similarly, during my term as mayor of Taipei, my administration made reducing the budget deficit and city government debt top objectives. Appealing for private sector adoption and volunteer involvement to help resolve social problems by reducing the city government burden, we did just what we set out to do, succeeding in our mission.

Another tenet of Drucker's management philosophy has given me tremendous inspiration. Analyzing the social welfare policies of such nations as the United States, Great Britain, Germany, and Italy, Drucker holds that Western social welfare systems are not performing their job, and that instead of cultivating self-reliance and strength, these systems have created extensive dependence, in turn shackling these nations with a tremendous social welfare burden. This is why Drucker praises the U.S. government's approach in the 1990s, in which the president encourages citizens to take up the volunteer movement and government budget is allocated to the private sector in order to promote social welfare measures. The volunteer movement having taken hold, a full 90 million American adults (half the population) are now serving in various capacities as volunteers, devoting an average of three hours per week of their time. Compared to the government, America's 900,000 volunteer organizations are twice as efficient. Not only have they helped strengthen social welfare measures, while successfully reducing fiscal pressure on the government, more importantly **the average American thinks of volunteering as a part of life, and gains a sense of self-realization and accomplishment from volunteering.**

Counting on government power alone to energize a civil society is far from enough. Instead, private sector departments must assist community renewal. This department is founded upon the involvement of volunteers and the caring of society. I agree with Drucker's point that "volunteers are the community," for the two go hand in hand, proving that the volunteer movement and community development must be conducted simultaneously to truly succeed.

In the month following the September 21 earthquake, I flew from Taipei to central Taiwan nearly every day to understand the situation first-hand and to employ every resource available in the relief effort. In the wake of the disaster, Taiwan's military, police, fire department, and medical personnel threw themselves into relief work, moving me deeply. Especially notable is that no serious public safety-related incidents broke out, once again demonstrating that Taiwan is a place of law and order. Moreover, the involvement of countless volunteer groups, whether organized, ad hoc, or individuals, is particularly inspiring. Among these groups, religious groups and charity organizations distinguished themselves with their performance and thorough efficiency, proving that Taiwanese society is full of decency and compassion.

It is said, "Righteousness gives nations plenty of friends, evil is the people's shame." The September 21 earthquake gave the value system of the Taiwanese people a huge shock. The Taiwanese, inured to living amidst plenty and stability, are now forced to consider the meaning and value of life on a deeper level. **The earthquake has convinced me that "volunteer Taiwan" and the "new Taiwanese family" should be incorporated into our society's value system.**

"Volunteer Taiwan" will be the engine for rebuilding the "new Taiwanese family." Volunteers are the community —the third department (social department) in addition to government (public department) and business (private department). With mission as the top priority, volunteers stress operational performance and thorough utilization of the community's human resources. However, this must begin with the learning, development, and self-validation of every individual. In addition, we should pay our respects to the power of women, the glue that binds the community together and the catalyst that brings it to life.

Once "volunteer Taiwan" becomes a new force in the private sector, we must pay special attention to the leadership and management of the volunteer movement, learning how to raise and utilize resources more effectively. Led by Dr. Lee Yuan-tseh, president of Academia

Sinica, the involvement of the private sector and the academic community in post-earthquake relief efforts, along the lines of religious groups, is an excellent example of intellectuals coming out of their laboratories and studies to get involved at the local level. The outpouring of diverse strength, coming from the religious and intellectual communities, points to Taiwan's vitality and exemplifies the essence of Young Taiwan.

Social construction according to female thinking

The strength of Taiwan's private volunteer force has grown tremendously in the past several years as participants come not only from religious backgrounds but also from the academic community, business community, as well as selfless school and community moms. The question on everyone's mind is, ' Taiwan is no longer poor, but what should we do now (or how shall we do it) to make Taiwan into a society marked by fairness, equality, community autonomy, and cultural diversity, thereby forging stronger social unity. From the Taipei Experience I learned to think of these issues from a female's perspective, for doing so can bring about unexpectedly perfect solutions.

For ages, Taiwanese society has made the female half of the population feel cold, and that no one cares how much pressure they are under at work, how overburdened by housework they are, how inhumane is their responsibility for looking after the young, old, and infirm, how insecure economic dependence makes them feel, and how unfair competitive conditions are to them out in society. While harsh competition may have set the model for Taiwan's economic advantage at this time, the injustice and wrongdoing that follows has triggered disorder and dampened our lives. Women especially, as the main victims of violent crime, are worried about burglars entering their homes or getting mugged out on the street. These problems can be traced to the widening gap between rich and poor. Rather than being based on equal attention and care, public policy is infected with an attitude that the disadvantaged should just as well disappear. This has created a lot of anger among a lot of people, so that the situation can easily get out of hand. In order to improve this hurtful environment, the government structure and policy thinking must incorporate the values typically associated with women—such as care, concern, communication, equality, and mutual trust and assistance —to forge a nation of, by, and for both sexes.

As mayor of Taipei, I placed female thinking into my municipal administrative plan, establishing a participatory democratic consultative mechanism for Taipei citizens. Operating smoothly, it got rave reviews from community members. To the city government organization, we added various cross-departmental decision-making bodies such as the Women's Rights Promotion Committee, to ensure thorough, comprehensive attention to issues. In the community, we teamed up with community members to promote the Community Environment Improvement Plan and Community Public Safety Conference, letting the people who understand the community best plan and protect their own community. We worked with private sector welfare groups on daycare issues, using classrooms and athletic fields in each school district's elementary schools to provide high quality, inexpensive after-school classes. This way, in one fell swoop we were able to solve the daycare worries of countless double income households, while taking children caught between school and empty homes off the streets.

One day, curious to see a Community Public Safety Conference in action, I visited the Wu Chang Community to see what it was all about. That day's discussion focused on finding blind spots in public safety. Community mothers had drawn a large map, and everyone clattering away at once as they pointed here and there on the map, they showed representatives from the police department the areas they thought were security blind spots. Their concerns were handed over to the police, the ward chief, and participating Neighborhood Watch merchants to undertake. Following the map, community police began patrolling, and within just a few days they surrounded most-wanted criminal Lin Chun-sheng on Wu Chang Street, accelerating the resolution of the country's most scrutinized criminal case ---- the kidnapping murder of Pai Hsiao-yen, daughter of celebrity Pai Pingping. Who could imagine that one's own community could defend itself with its own power ?

The seemingly trivial issue of "daycare service" deserves a good look, too. Thanks to the community spirit of equality,universality, and autonomy, this undertaking can maximize the return on social costs. First, children and the elderly received excellent care, allowing the adult population —especially women —to work in confidence outside the community, contributing to their families and society at large. Second, each person received impartial caring and the attention they needed. This way, maintaining an optimal mental and physical state, people can perform at their best and contribute at their maximum to their country and society. Similarly, good care can help prevent people filled with rancor generated by a lifetime of scarcity from getting desperate and taking desperate measures, or from perpetually engaging in mean-spirited competition out of fear for lacking, lining their own pockets at a cost. Third, community autonomy benefits consensus throughout society, and can reduce the administrative cost of formulating and executing policy, eliminating resistance and homing in on the people's needs, and ensuring maximal administrative results. Fourth, the community involvement planning model promoted in Taipei gets to the root of public safety, the issue of highest concern among Taiwanese at this time, for this model can be considered "bolstering police administration with social policy."

Such social policies, aimed at achieving social stability and prosperity, are vital tools helping a nation progress towards lasting peace and prosperity. In essence, it means building fewer prisons and more daycare centers. For a place such as Taiwan, urgently needing social unity, while depending heavily on foreign trade and facing fierce trade competition in the global arena, it is imperative to maintain the caliber of the population, as well as the cohesiveness and vitality of society. Where these issues are concerned, we can learn a few things from the female way of thinking that might help us find a route to survival.

The aging of the population and the weakening of the function of the family are worldwide issues in the 21st century. I believe that in today's Taiwan such issues as caring for children and the elderly, restoring family values, and maintaining a secure living environment are the most critical issues demanding appropriate solutions. They also happen to be the issues about which women are most personally concerned and are best at handling. This is why we should expand democracy to the female population, designing assorted avenues for women to join in formulating sound public policy on these issues, then put them into action. This way, we allow women to put their characteristic capacity for "keeping an eye on the wallet," ensuring maximal application of government and private funding. In sum, putting women's experiences and talents to work cannot be overlooked as a valuable means for resolving the tough issues of the new era.

Recently I discovered that, the community public safety and community childcare programs the city government supervised in conjunction with public departments and private sector strength —in which women were instrumental in communication, decision-making, and administration —have been introduced in Taipei County, Kaohsiung City, Kaohsiung County, and Tainan City, each administrative districts where the DPP is the ruling party. Furthermore, in the aftermath of the September 21 earthquake, the Peng Wan-ru Foundation, long a leading proponent of the community daycare model, took the Taipei experience into the disaster area, and in very short order (commencing planning in October and operation in November), has already begun to provide after-school care for several hundred children from five elementary schools in the hard-hit areas of Tungshih and Puli. I have also learned that similar services will commence shortly in remote areas such as Chungliao. In Puli, the same community public safety model will be expanded into caring for the elderly and the infirm in their own homes.

I am quite gratified with this news, for on the one hand it helps prove that the experiments we conducted in Taipei City are suitable for all of Taiwan, including even remote areas. On the other hand, I am confident that these sorts of developments demonstrate the power of the Taiwanese people and their hope for the future.

More and more people are getting involved as volunteers in community and welfare work or culture and arts events. This self-motivated force shows the way to hope for Taiwan. After all, we do not live on this land simply to extract momentary benefits, but to invest our lives in a worthwhile future.

Confidence, trust, and faith

My second trip to Japan to learn about restoration work in the aftermath of the Osaka-Kobe earthquake deeply impressed upon me that, in addition to institutional development, "spiritual restoration" should be undertaken at the same time. As I see it, "spiritual restoration" can be approached on three levels:

1. **Restoring self-confidence.** The September 21 earthquake was one of the most devastating disasters in Taiwanese history, yet somehow it stirred the people's confidence, hopes, and kindness. Through constant contact with all sorts of people throughout society, I have found that many people's perspectives on life have changed, from concern with "what they have" to "what they have given." One volunteer put it this way to me, saying "As long as you give, you won't feel powerless, for once you give of yourself life is much

fuller." This description, spoken out of intense personal experience, underscores the importance of confidence, for confidence gives us the courage to face the tangible destruction wrought by disaster.

2. **Restoring trust in others.** "Trust" is a basic ingredient for advancement to a civil society. Facing the earthquake together, people's trust in others grew, embodying the compassion of Jesus' exhortation to "love thy neighbor." In the effort to foster the interactive relationship between "trust" and "covenants," I proposed that government authorities should formulate a special law to act as the legal basis for crisis response. Meanwhile, "shareholder relations" and "partnerships" based on mutual trust should be re-established between the central government and local governments, as well as government and the private sector. It is this sort of trust that emerges as so vital whenever disaster has struck.

3. **Restore faith in the land.** Taiwan used to be plagued with tensions related to place of birth, ethnic background, and party affiliation, but the earthquake strengthened feelings of shared destiny, and created a new interpretation of identification with the land. Post-disaster restoration made people certain that we must rebuild the ideal of a "pure land." This kind of faith, an extension of identification with the land, is collective power; it is the antidote to ethnic differences, family background, and party affiliation, and a new popular orientation that politicians must appreciate.

Following the September 21 earthquake I truly felt the regenerative power of Taiwan's civilization, the people's zest for social justice, their concern for the poor and the victims of disasters. The establishment of such new relationships between people and others, people and the earth, and people and nature, have rapidly taken Taiwan from a "me" era to an "us" era, which can only be good news for Taiwan's future.

"A reed crushed by a weight will not break; a flickering lantern does not go out." The love of others lights up the room, the love of the people builds on itself, so bright it outshines the sun. This is the unlimited potential of collective love.

The marriage of wisdom and virtue

Vincent Van Gogh once said, "The earth nourished me for 30 years. Full of thanks, I want to leave some souvenirs for her." Having perceived the meaning of life, Van Gogh threw himself totally into painting, leaving precious spiritual assets for all of human civilization.

After leaving my position as mayor of Taipei on 25 December 1998, I retreated to tranquility for some quiet reflection, then stopped to consider what I should do next. Van Gogh's self-exhortation is mine, too, for **I am grateful to Taiwan, the land and its people.**

Being thankful requires learning, and in turn learning requires penetrating the grass roots, and assimilating the inner essence of Taiwan. The grass roots are my background, and I must give of myself, repaying the soil that gave me the gift of life.

Spurred by this kind of motivation, I embarked upon a study tour consisting of a "learning journey," a "journey into the land," and "industrial journey, learning and caring on one hand, while thinking and reflecting on my own situation. Through close interaction with the people and the land, I was deeply struck by the fact that to become a successful politician one must care and must possess the ability to engage in broad, far-reaching reflection on philosophy, religion, and personality. Caring, one may then look for the wisdom with which to dedicate to the land and people of Taiwan.

This is the most basic, yet the most stringent requirement for a national leader.

This period of learning and reflection helped me to reaffirm my determination to be a politician, my caring, and the means to deliver this caring. Over this year's time, I felt myself growing and maturing once again. Politics has never been an easy pursuit. Greek philosopher Aristotle believed that leaders must have the following qualities: courage, an even-tempered disposition, restraint, goodness, generosity, honesty, esteem, solemnity, playfulness, humor, and a sense of righteousness. Who knows how much more complex today's politics is compared to that of ancient Greece. And who knows how much more wisdom is required from today's politicians than the qualities noted by Aristotle.

I often think back at my personal growth, from a country boy to today, and remind myself that I cannot cease learning henceforth. A politician in the new era must possess the mind of a philosopher, religious figure, and artist, growing in heart and mind with the people at every moment, and constantly pursing excellence together with the people.

Together with the people of this land, apart from pursuing success in the conventional sense, I want to seek meaning and value in life. Taking on responsibility in order to serve society, fostering the habit of respecting others, cultivating self-esteem and self-regulation, having the courage to tap into potential and creativity, casting off the constraints of outmoded thinking, and leaving the "limited" to pursue the "unlimited." All Taiwanese must remember that we are all sons and daughters of the land —sons and daughters of Taiwan.

Reflecting on the foundation of the New Middle Road, I have come to appreciate that global reality under the new order is different from the Cold War period model of antagonism. We must take a broader perspective of the world to eliminate antagonistic positions, and by accepting others' perspectives and comparing the differences, we can look for a higher level of appreciation. This way, while maintaining our own position, we can use persuasion to make the other side reevaluate their viewpoint and readjust thinking towards achieving a win-win situation. Based on this understanding, we can see that new leadership means finding balance between opposite extremes, and tapping into societal consensus. The political paths of Bill Clinton and Tony Blair demonstrate that the "Third Way" and "New Middle Road" represent new thinking in response to globalization, localization, changes in individual lifestyles, and relationships between people and society as well as between humans and nature.

Changing the current black-gold political nexus, and continuing to forge "new Taiwan —energetic government," Taiwan must experience a changing of the guard from one political party to another so as to break up the unyielding political-economic interest structure.

With this in mind, I have placed the focus of the Taiwanese version of the "Third Way" —the New Middle Road —on national security, the termination of black-gold politics, alternating political power between different political parties, restoring our home, and cultivating great love for Taiwan. I have grouped these ideas, the sum of my observations and thinking over the past several years, under the single motto "The New Taiwanese Family, New Hope in the Millennium."

Like Martin Luther King, I have a dream. My dream involves opening the door to alternating central government majority power, and from there, together with people of all different ideals and corners of society, **building a new society characterized by righteousness, compassion, law and order, while preparing for the challenges of the new century.** I am sure that the majority of the people on the island of Taiwan share this dream. In order to realize this dream, the government's top job is to provide opportunities for fair development, to strengthen people's awareness of self-responsibility through education, and stride forward to wards a righteous society in which relationships between people are founded upon trust. In the words of the Jewish prophet Micah, "Do justly, love mercy, and walk humbly with your God."Back when we said "go for it!" we threw ourselves into politics for this shared dream. And in all the years since that time, this part has never changed.

Chapter Nine

Sweeping National Security

Taiwan does not sail on smooth seas. The formulation and execution of policy by the "ship's captain" has a momentous impact on the nation's future security. A far-reaching perspective helps put risks from all sides under control. This is where a national leader's foremost concerns lie. Whether in national security, which outranks all other issues in importance, economic security as the engine of sustained development, or the baseline safety net of security in society, I am pleased to offer my thinking and perceptions here for others to consider.

Risks and security: issues of survival

Each time I look back on my personal growth process —from a background of poverty, to fighting hard to come out ahead in competition for entry into each level of schooling; to abandoning business for law, and law for politics; from elected representative to administrative chief of the nation's capital —throughout this process, assuming different roles, and faced with different challenges, pressure has been a constant presence. Through it all, apart from always trying to make prompt decisions, learning and thinking have always been a great motivator for my growth.

However, the real turning points in my life have had the deepest impact on me. During the period I practiced maritime commerce law, the 1970s, Taiwan's export trade exploded. In my capacity, I pondered how to resolve my clients' trade disputes. Through my practice, I came to appreciate the importance of an export-oriented economy for Taiwan's development. Even today, import and export trade account for a major slice of the GDP pie, such that trade can be thought of as Taiwan's lifeblood. Soon thereafter, having joined the opposition movement and gotten involved in politics, I experienced and witnessed the democratization process, seeing ever more clearly that unless the ruling party steps down and yields to another party and the organized crime-big money nexus isn't broken apart, Taiwan's economic accomplishments will be eroded away. In addition, constantly flip-flopping cross-straits policy not only threatens national security, but also makes Taiwan directionless on the global competitive stage. Special attention to national security as a legislator, and city diplomacy as mayor has helped me see that Taiwan's survival and development are full of unpredictability and challenge. Personally, I am glad for the opportunity to have grown together with Taiwan. Over nearly half a century of history, I have been involved in many of the important reforms. I never forget for a moment that this is a gift from fate. Young people have asked me, 'What is the secret to success?' And while I don't know if what I am today can be considered a success, I know for sure that an individual can adjust to the challenges thrown at him by the greater environment through diligent study or expanding his breadth of thought. However, if we have higher expectations of ourselves, we shouldn't be satisfied with just our ability to adjust. Changing with the surroundings like a chameleon is one strategy for survival, but management and adaptation practiced according to outdated information only lets you get by in easy times. Always finding comfort in whatever comes one's way is no way to turn challenges into opportunities, not to mention changing the greater environment.

If Taiwan is a ship, we are not sailing along on calm inland waters; on the contrary, we must confront the massive ocean swells, as risk and danger lurk at all times. We do not lack opportunity, but faced with risks, it is imperative that we anticipate opportunities and engage in proactive risk-related policy decisions. With this in mind, I have proposed the New Middle Road, with national security at the core, as my platform in the 2000 presidential election with an eye toward the comprehensive and proactive risk-related policy-making Taiwan needs today.

Risk-related policy-making is not passive management and

reaction, nor is it just relief measures in the aftermath of disasters. If we can think a bit more and analyze potential risk factor, and anticipate the way such risks may spread, we can come up with preventative approaches, or perhaps turn a given situation into an opening. We can even take action to dissipate risk, turning it into an opportunity. The concept of prevention over treatment can be applied in many ways beyond the treatment of illness: **analysis and assessment of risks in advance save costs compared to post-facto remedies.**

While presiding over Taipei City government administration, many dangerous public structures required reinforcement or demolition/rebuilding, demanding a great deal of thought. The lack of general familiarity toward the concept of risk policy formulation made execution extra difficult, but analysis and assessment in advance enabled timely action. Without prior evaluation, the impact of a disaster such as the September 21 earthquake would have been unimaginable. Thus, advance prevention and warning will become the core of risk policy formulation in the future.

For risk analysis and assessment to be comprehensive takes more than government officials enlisting the help of a few scholars and expert;, for it takes much farther-reaching participation, encompassing the views and concerns of private groups and members of society at large. Inclusion of a broader cross-section of participants not only helps form more complete analysis and policy formation, but can also advance the elevation of the population's risk awareness in general. In other words, **the private sector and government team up in partnership to analyze risks, react to change, and take up responsibility together. This is the optimal model for Taiwan to**

face crises and challenges in the future. In addition, how to handle assessed risks and how to invest limited resources in prevention are critical issues. Taking a buckshot approach to risk investment is not only ineffectual —not to mention lacking forethought on policy —but serves as a negative example of wasted resources.

To take this concept further, comprehensive and proactive risk-related policy-making is the core of collective security. **Today's global community handles tasks such as environmental protection, technology and commerce, or disaster, crime and warfare, through various global avenues.** As the whole gamut of issues and events — good and bad —is proliferated via international channels, no nation can go about its business in complete isolation from the world, nor can countries believe that only they know best or can work independently on regional or even global issues. The importance of multi-national cooperation cannot be overlooked.

Take for the example Thailand's economic crisis in 1997, which swept through East Asian nations including Malaysia, Singapore, Indonesia, and even highly industrialized South Korea, like a plague. This occurred because opportunists seized on the weaknesses of the financial structure and in one blow practically wiped out the fruits of the last decade of efforts by these East Asian nations. So devastating was the crisis that today, over two years later, some countries are still not out of the woods. Although Taiwan does not enjoy a very good diplomatic situation today, there is still a lot that can be done. In particular, neighborhood diplomacy with multi-national risk management at the core is one area well worth pursuing.

Risks and security appear to run counter to one another, yet there are actually many shared dynamics between them. In the world in which we live, nothing has ever been guaranteed 100 percent safe, but what can be done is reducing risks. This is why our discussion of security at present refers to comprehensive and effective risk management in advance, expending resources according to the proportional risks, making improvements, and lowering risks. This comprehensive and aggressive definition of security is the kind of security that can be assured.

To me, evaluating all kinds of risks and anticipating all sorts of eventualities is what security is about. This is why **I believe that national security encompasses several fundamental levels: defense security, economic security, and social security. Defense security is the foundation of national security, safeguarding the basics like citizens' lives and property, and protecting our democratic system. Economic security involves how to establish and maintain advantage amidst global industry competition, maintaining Taiwan's economic vitality and prosperity. Social security is founded upon cultural, intellectual, and volunteer resources, transforming care for the disadvantaged into social resources so that they can rejoin the productive forces of society.**

These three aspects must all be taken care of at the same time. This way, the concept of advance warning is incorporated in each aspect, so that management and decision-making concerning risk can be fully implemented. Especially today, in a time when Taiwan faces a succession of challenges in the new century, we must look to the people to put aside their prejudices, no matter what their age or occupation, and take a more open-minded, forward-looking approach to contemplating Taiwan's problems. Confronting the risks of the future together, national security can be preserved.

National security outranks all else

Taiwan's most direct difficulties come from relations across the Taiwan Strait with China. Naturally, the media and political figures often focus on cross-strait issues. Despite this concern and focus, however, subjective elements such as national status, pro-independence or —unification ideology, and even ethnic identity all come in to play, supplanting rational analysis and leading to sloppy judgment. The most commonly observed situation is that groups with pro-unification leanings presume that military invasion of Taiwan is China's only viable option, so the foremost consideration overriding both internal and external issues is not angering China. Similar situations can be observed in certain pro-independence groups who, driven by their beliefs, think that with Taiwan under the protective umbrella of the United States, China will not attempt to use force against Taiwan. While there are elements of truth in each stance, both sides over-simplify the possibilities. Placing critical state business within one-sided assumptions and over-simplified presumptions is extremely dangerous. I have always believed that when it comes to a serious issue such as national security, it is better to fret a bit more, ponder a bit more, deduce, and analyze a bit more to prepare for any eventuality.

Any confrontation is like a game of chess, as we might not be able to predict our opponent's moves. If we are rational enough, then we must carefully survey the entire board for a clear look at where we stand in relation to our opponent. From there, considering what pieces and moves are available to our opponent, we can calculate his strategies and tactics and see his true objectives clearly. Having achieved this, we can then investigate the most advantageous approach for us, evaluating the game with each development, and turn it into the most advantageous situation for us. This is why **Taiwan cannot afford to be quixotic concerning any opponent, nor can we let them dictate our position;** rather, we must anticipate all their possible reactions and formulate comprehensive strategic countermeasures. From the softest to the hardest, the most ideal to the worst situations, only by having a full store of strategic countermeasures can we formulate good policies to cover the full spectrum of possibilities.

For Taiwan, cross-strait issues, national defense, and diplomacy are intertwined together in a trinity, each affecting the other. China is the greatest military threat to Taiwan at this time and also the greatest impediment and antagonist on the diplomatic front. China is so hostile towards Taiwan, using these two pliers to squeeze Taiwan, because China has no confidence in its ability to attain Taiwan with the "one country, two systems" model. She then presumes that diplomatic conduct and military threats can turn Taiwan into a child incapable of any behavior or defense,except just doing what he is told. This has always been the wishful thinking of certain mythmakers. But is Taiwan really a child? In this case, we must establish a deep-structured defensive military to use as a front line of defense. In addition early warning diplomacy to prevent miscalculation, can keep Taiwan from getting pinched.

Before China's mythmakers begin to see beyond historical myths, the last thing we want to see is a military conflict between China and Taiwan. Yet that does not mean we cannot take defensive precautions, because the way our confused adversaries think, the use of force depends entirely on the myth, and the objective of their reverie: all means used to achieve the unification of Taiwan can be adjusted at any time to meet this objective. They claim that their refusal to renounce the use of force against Taiwan is directed at foreign forces, but this is a semantic game under their myth, because the Taiwan Strait is most certainly not Chinese inland waters, and foreign forces and interests have long been involved in Taiwan. Therefore, according to the terms of the mythmakers, they have a ready justification to use force at any time. Whether or not to use force is a question of chances of success and the costs involved; if everything favored the mythmakers, they would make their move right now without hesitation.

In terms of military behavior, Taiwan must foster the concept of deep-level defense. In addition to augmenting advance warning reconnaissance to China's Nanjing and Guangzhou military regions, calculating all possibilities of military conduct at all times in line with military deployments in order to prevent unmatched military power in the Taiwan Strait, we must exchange intelligence with nations in the region to head off the chances of China's adventurism. Meanwhile, we must establish a mechanism for cross-strait security dialogue, taking all steps necessary to prevent miscalculation based in illusion from precipitating conflict and spreading beyond control.

Advance warning diplomacy must employ goodwill to expand

formal and informal mechanisms of engagement. Its scope should cover concerned nations in the region (Apart from China and the United States, this must also include Japan, as well as East Asian nations such as the Philippines and Korea.) At this time, given the scarcity of diplomatic opportunities based on recognition of sovereignty, Taiwan must promote good neighbor diplomacy based on risk management. Motivated by collective military and security considerations, concerned regional nations will surely be willing to maintain substantive relations with Taiwan regarding regional security. Moreover, with shared interests in mind, they are likely to cooperate and take action. I believe this is an excellent way to make diplomacy a natural defensive screen.

China's threat towards Taiwan is rooted in Chinese nationalism. Chinese nationalism has a solid supporting structure with a fragile core. The solid support comes from its social foundation, as China has a group of fanatical nationalists close enough to the power center to impact decision making. They advocate zero softness on the "Taiwan issue," and not relinquishing the use of military force against Taiwan (China's military recruitment system ensures that these people are free from the direct risk of going to battle.)

Nevertheless, Chinese nationalism has a fragile core, because the foundation of nationalism is emotional, with no tangible interests at stake other than abstract interests. Thus, the natural enemy of emotional nationalism is "interests" —tangible, not abstract interests. Sovereign interests are abstract, all-or-nothing interests (you either win or you lose), while such interests as trade or transportation routes are tangible, allowing for winners on two or more sides. What kind of interests can be used to lobby? For instance, China can be made to realize that her true interests lie in East Asia, not in Taiwan, thus engendering a directional shift in China's foreign policy toward a win-win track for China and Taiwan and a multi-win line for the nations of East Asia. This is why making out a balance sheet of tangible interests for China and East Asia is clearer and potentially more convincing to China than a ledger of debts and assets defined in terms of abstract sovereignty.

Granted, given the greater global strategic chess board, we understand that with Taiwan's strategic location, we could easily become the object of a turf war or a pawn of the superpowers in the ongoing covert conflicts and overt tensions between the U.S. and China. Not just for Taiwan, but among East Asia's various nations, the potential of getting caught in the crossfire between two large foes is a difficult issue.

On the other hand, the interests of East Asia are closely tied together with China's coastal region; especially China's southeastern coastal region which shares interests with Taiwan. Whether in terms of abstract sovereignty or military threats, neither poses tangible interests for China. Specifically, this sort of situation is an opportunity for China, in its role as an East Asian trading power, to let go of historical bitterness and bring sincerity to bear in preventing the nations of East Asia from becoming trapped in a consuming spiral of mutual defense. The blue highway of China's seaboard is the lifeblood of East Asia's nations, as well as the core of the East Asian economic sphere. Rather than controlling the strait, threatening the navigation routes of neighboring countries, it would be better to extend these waters to them to make them feel secure, thereby consolidating China's trading status in East Asia. If China relinquishes this opportunity, putting the nations of East Asia into a state of internal depletion and mutual suspicion and scheming, Oriental civilization will forfeit the historical chance, under China's leadership, to become a leading civilization in the 21st century.

If China, as the great power of East Asia, wishes to pull equal weight to the United States on the world stage, she must alter her ideology, completely relinquishing designs of territorial occupation in favor of strategic thinking with ideological appropriation at its core. The wisdom of the Chinese saying "The benevolent have no enemies, those with no appetite for killing draw the people to their side," not only applies to personal cultivation, but is even more useful for true "conquerors." The uncontested supremacy of the United States today could not be sustained with military power alone. Its most amazing aspect is that it makes the world believe that Americans live well, thus they wish to be American. I hope China understands this distinction, or as the Yuan empire illustrates, no matter how much land or people under your dominion, sole reliance on military hegemony cannot be sustained for too long.

Of course, persuasion is never easy, but it is truly the way to take care of a drastic situation. If we can give consideration to the social component that supports nationalism, we can build an appeal to China structured on lucid calculation and clear analysis of interests at stake. This is something that the ruling Kuomintang has failed to think of, and a way for the DPP to demonstrate the scope of its roadmap for state governance.

I have always believed that working on a foundation of goodwill and equality, Taiwan and China should pursue mutual interests and together forge an advantageous for all. This is one of the reasons why , if elected president, I hope to make a visit to China before taking office.

Economic security:
the engine of sustained development

Foreign construction workers and domestic helpers are busy on our construction sites and in our homes, fashionable attire comes from France and Italy, the lobster at the seafood stand comes from Argentina, Japanese ramen noodle shops, and even American specialty coffee chain Starbucks have all made tremendous inroads into Taiwan. Taiwan produces cloth for a French clothing design, manufactured in Macao, and computers for American brands on an OEM basis. This influx and outflow of personnel, materials, currency, information, and technology signifies Taiwan's entry into the age of globalization.

In a sense, globalization is a historical experience for Taiwan. Western colonialism was the first wave of globalization, a period during which Taiwan was given the appellation *Ilha Formosa*, "beautiful island," by Portuguese in the Western Pacific. I recall a popular Hoklo language song from my childhood in Tainan, "Anping Reminiscence," about a young woman of Dutch parentage, sitting by the harborside in the old Taiwanese capital city of Anping (today's Tainan), pining for her man.

Confronting this new condition, we must analyze all contributing factors and formulate timely responses. In my view, the process of globalization affects us on four levels:

1. **Natural environmental avenues:** energy, material, and living resources are transmitted.
2. **Transportation avenues:** Human beings created various communication networks for transporting personnel and materials and engage in trade.
3. **Capital avenues:** The commercial structure developed the financial system with currency as the basis of exchange. Today's multinational capital flow often outweighs international trade by 10, even 100 times over.
4. **Information avenues:** Today, digital information in the form of bits has become the sole standard of information transmission. The capacity to transmit information over long distances has increased the volume of information transmission thousands of times over the conventional telephone, forming the basis of today's intellectual economy and Internet commerce.

Different avenues have different characteristics and convey different things. But these channels and avenues for the circulation of people, materials, currency, information, and technology all share the quality of standardization. Standardization can reduce the costs of communication and transportation, enabling interchange beyond a nation's borders and geographic barriers, while also having **the advantage of economy of scale**, constantly expanding its global scope due to its innate propensity for expansion. This process is known as globalization.

The driving force behind the tide of globalization is the human capacity for utilizing material resources. Working through the mechanism of market exchange, the less adveloped areas utilize the advantage of lower cost labor, gradually receiving the results of growth from advanced areas. In fact, the overspill of economic growth dominates the entire rise and development of capitalism.

Mercantilism, the precursor of capitalism, originated in Venice, a town that grew out of a fishing village. Employing an advanced commercial network coupled with navigational expertise, the Venetians made their way from Rome to Holland and Spain, forging the rise of a maritime hegemon. It was during this time that Taiwan encountered Western civilization for the first time. Following the Industrial Revolution, nations wielding advanced technology, such as Britain, France, and Germany, established colonial strongholds around the globe in what can be considered the first instance of the globalization of capitalism.

With the establishment of the New World of North America, capitalism gained a new engine in the form of material energy and systemic organization, through which the United States established its superpower status after the Second World War.

The entire historical process of capitalism is simply the transmission of economic fluctuations from advanced areas to backward areas via transportation avenues. Closer to home, the flourishing development of process-and-export areas in the 1960s and 1970s, in line with the formation of the Cold War order, marked Taiwan's first appearance on the stage of globalization, becoming a contestant as one of Asia's "Four Little Dragons." At the time, I was practicing law as maritime commerce attorney, handling a large volume of disputes arising from import-export trade.

Since that time, the dissolution of the Soviet bloc, the collapse of the Cold War structure, the economic development of Eastern Europe, and the rapid growth of China's coastal regions, have all transpired for the same reasons. We see the rapid increase in the world's contestants, reshaping the face of things while presenting an even greater test of Taiwan's economic status. Naturally, such rapid development does not come without a price, as the depletion of resources, destruction of nature, and the environment's capacity for tolerance remain natural limitations on economic fluctuations.

Taking the example of the trans-national economic crisis of 1997, the soft underbelly of the East Asian financial structure was struck by opportunists, nearly destroying almost a decade of hard work by the various affected nations. This example shows that global avenues not only transmit environmental protection, technology, and commerce, but can also carry disaster, crime, and war, as even greater interests come with even greater risks. On this new stage, only world-class contestants are welcome, causing the world's nations to tread lightly to avoid becoming spare tires or getting taken out of action too soon. This is why global risk management and related policy making should be a vital issue in the 21st century. If we can grasp developmental trends, we can anticipate opportunities, familiarize ourselves with the modes of global development, and even foresee its future scope.

The world globalization survival strategy: lacking the

advantage of size, one must ;leverage strengths to achieve success against the big players. This is why the winners in the global economy must have a system to improve efficiency. They must establish industrial policy oriented toward global competitiveness, raise productivity, capture the relative advantage of horizontal and vertical division of labor while helping industry secure low-risk financial capital in the global industrial system, and claim a margin of profit amidst the fluctuations of the global economy.

Global competition brings with it industry exodus and unemployment, the risks of which the government must bear. The sum of the unemployment rate, inflation rate and other indicators comprises the misery index [17], a tool employed by countries to gauge the people's suffering and conduct risk management. Especially given the global reshuffling of economic power, pinching Taiwan between the three major economic blocs of Europe, the Americas, and Asia, Taiwan must respond prudently, as over-dependence on resources, materials, labor, or markets from any particular region hinders economic risk management. Taiwan's expanding dependence on China's market and labor in recent years, while tossing a major unknown into the equation, is nonetheless seemingly inevitable in light of economic trends. In this situation, it is worth looking further into the issue of industry upgrade

---

[17] The misery index rates living conditions according to 10 indices of human welfare: life expectancy, daily calorie supply, clean drinking water, infant immunization, secondary school enrollment, per capita GNP, inflation, communications technology, political freedom, and civil rights. (Additional measures considered include data on pollution, unemployment, external debt, children in the work force, urban slums, income distribution, infant mortality, physicians per capita, literacy, and access to consumer goods.) The index was created to measure, in a single figure, differences in living conditions among various countries.

in Taiwan.

On the cusp of the new millennium, technology-intensive and capital-intensive industries now form the mainstream of Taiwanese industry. However, nationwide investment in research and development is relatively low, and beyond such hot industries as information electronics, communications, and semiconductors, current incentive policies aimed at industry upgrade remain insufficient. Consequently, to borrow a sports metaphor, in the global competition of industry, lacking sufficient R&D "bench depth," Taiwan can only go with the flow and is ill equipped to take the lead. **In order to promote industry upgrade and government reformation beneficial to all sides, Taiwan must establish the following strategic objectives amidst global competition:**

1. **Consolidate the state's fiscal foundation:** Under pressure to upgrade and to reap capital profit, the average wage gap across industries is widening. Meanwhile, pressured by consumption and taxation, industry operator savings are on the decline. And with the function of individual savings weakened, dependence on state welfare expenditure is inevitable. When this happens, the state will be like any industry. If it is unable to improve operations and raise competitiveness, the state will be unable to pay out growing welfare benefits. Meanwhile, the expanded cost of welfare benefits and liability could precipitate a state credit (in liabilities) and trust (in welfare) crisis. With this in mind, responsible agencies must disclose quarterly income and expenditures, hold open hearings for all quarters of society to discuss welfare policy planning, and then elucidate in detail to the citizenry by the media to demonstrate the

appropriateness of welfare policy planning.

2. **Promote "leading departments," review "lagging departments," abolish "redundant departments," attack "harmful departments:** Both industry and government share a fundamental affliction in that they are unwilling to admit the existence of these four types of departments in their respective "households." As a result, leading departments are held back, lagging departments are ignored, redundant departments are sustained, and harmful departments are indulged. State leaders must distinguish between these four categories, consider a broad range of opinions, and engage in comparative evaluation before undertaking reform, so as to establish the right conditions for the next step in industry development.

3. **Strengthen the flow of outstanding talent towards R&D:** Under this approach, the government identifies outstanding individuals in various academic disciplines to undergo special monthly training and receive generous financial support. Following a given number of years of service in a particular field, program participants are required to accept priority placement in government or private units with special needs. For their part, government and private sector units must announce short-term, mid-term, and long-term needs, and constantly separate the wheat from the chaff. This approach offers a means to break through the current plight of R&D in Taiwan, and achieve the objective of "keeping outstanding talents in Taiwan."

Given the near depletion of useable natural resources worldwide and judging from the transmission of economic fluctuations, economic growth produced via the exchange of materials is finite. Thus, humanity must confront the challenges of retrenched material consumption in the future. In other words, an alternative must be found to replace the economic growth model established upon material consumption.

In the future, satisfaction of human desires must shift from material satisfaction to spiritual satisfaction, and from "hardware" consumption to "software" consumption. Compared to the limitations on material economics by the capacity of the natural environment, the scope of the information economy is practically unlimited. The material world of this planet is finite, while the human spiritual universe is infinite.

This is why future modes of consumption will undoubtedly shift toward reduced material consumption, and rapidly increasing "spiritual" consumption. If we begin with the information economy, new economic growth will surely far exceed the scope established by the traditional material economy.

Global competition in the 21st century will center on human resources, technology, and capital. In the administration of a state, human resources are most important, followed by technology and capital in that order. Whoever can cultivate top caliber people and employ them wisely need not worry about technological enhancement or poor state management. National leaders must undertake a full inventory of historical assets and liabilities, developing the talents of individuals displaying the greatest potential in their respective fields.Next they must boost the competitiveness of the disadvantaged, while allowing the elimination of inefficient redundant personnel. Further, they must administrate policy based on investigative analysis of critical issues, and establish a healthy cycle for human resources, technology, and capital. Only by taking such steps, informed by wisdom and reinforced by daring and resolution, can they cut away the malignancy of the mafia-money order and greet the economic future of "new growth."

Social security as an underlying protective net

Growing up in a poor family has given me strong empathy for the plight of society's less fortunate people, and the desire to help them out of their poverty some day. Over the course of my political career, beginning with initial welfare concepts, I have had the opportunity to become familiar with the importance of establishing a broader social security system. I believe beyond poverty relief, civilized nations must employ the system of modern society to allow people to live safer, more secure lives. These social security systems form a buffer zone to help people confront what changes of fortune may come in life. In this capacity, the state can become the people's partner. A fine system to begin with, its intentions and methods are misunderstood by many people throughout society, which is why I have taken even more time to seek counsel from experts in related fields. I would like to share some of my conclusions here.

I believe that social security in a broader sense should encompass economic, employment, education, housing, public safety (especially the personal safety of women), and the scope normally thought of as "social welfare." Each of these realms affects the other, thus they must be considered together. For instance, employment and housing pressure drops under a good economy, and the crime rate declines as well, lifting pressure on social welfare outlays. However, the opposite can also occur, in which case social welfare expenditures become tight, hampering care for the disadvantaged while overall social security risks increase. Still, even under the best conditions, there will always be a set of disadvantaged people in society who, due to their relative lack of competitiveness, face difficulty in education and employment, making them a high-risk group in terms of crime. It is at times like this when social welfare becomes the final means of salvation, which is why I think of social welfare as a protective net underlying social security.

With this in mind, **social security can be simplified into three realms: First is support for the disadvantaged,** providing appropriate aid to the lower reaches of society to safeguard their basic rights to survival. **Next is helping everyone in society to resist unpredictable events in life,** such as illness, involuntary unemployment, or injuries suffered in the work place. **Third are safeguards during the childhood and elderly stages of life.** The purpose of this support is for community power and prior contributions to kick in when an individual is unable to contribute to production with his own power.

Surveying human history, we see that other than the early establishment of support for the disadvantaged, the second and third areas are approaches to mutual assistance developed in modern times. At first, individuals used savings to protect themselves, followed by the development of mutual assistance organizations. However, insufficient participation limited the effectiveness of the latter, ultimately leading to the development of modern social security structures marked by participation of all citizens nationwide. In other words, this kind of system was intended to make up for the inadequacies of random private organizations. However, having been instituted for half a century, European welfare systems are plagued by massive deficits, underscoring the importance of prudence in our pursuit of social security.

Generally speaking, huge budget deficits in social security systems largely stem from social welfare outlays. At the root lie two chief issues, the first being the combination of increased life spans and reduced birth rates. The system's original designers never anticipated the resulting massive shift in the age structure. Therefore, while the working population has decreased dramatically, social security payments to senior citizens cannot be reduced, causing structural debt. Second is the steep rise of medical costs. Having secured health insurance, people pay closer attention to health care and live longer lives, naturally generating the increase of overall outlays. Meanwhile, with the continual improvement and spiraling cost of medical equipment, given the limitation of resources, appropriate allotment of medical expenses becomes a priority issue for nations worldwide.

Today, as Taiwan enters the ranks of aging societies, methods selected to safeguard the lives of the elderly must be calculated rationally using population model predictions to revise risks. Among these methods, some should involve mandatory institution by the state, while another portion should include encouraging individual savings and investment. Ideally, the two approaches should go together. A key issue in the Kuomintang's current arrangement is that participation in the social security system is not mandated nationally for all citizens, and participants in insurance programs for military, civil servants, and teaching corps are free to choose among various programs. This can easily lead to special privilege for select groups, having a huge negative impact on the national insurance system. Learning from the examples of certain European nations, Taiwan must take care not to make similar mistakes.

Taiwan's health insurance system is also experiencing debt at this time. Evaluating the options before us, we hope to preserve the basic spirit of health insurance, but approve of adopting measures to combat waste and reduce the deficit. The most controversial aspect of Taiwan's current structure is that it raises certain burdens on consumers, while failing to work as hard to apply budgetary volume controls to healthcare providers. I believe that each concerned group under the health insurance system must take responsibility, working together with an appreciation for their respective partnerships to truly resolve deficit issues.

In advanced nations, retirement funds and health insurance outlays account for the majority of social welfare expenses. With this in mind, as Taiwan maps out its social welfare system, we must pay particular attention to these two systems. Furthermore, we must also note that in addition to the assorted support payments under the welfare system (such as stipends for children and unemployment), inexpensive educational costs also comprise an important support measure, not only ensuring the education of the majority, but enabling the laboring population to learn a second skill. As the saying goes, "it is better to teach him how to make a net than give him fish to eat," and the conventional wisdom of the population has already pointed the way for social welfare. Consequently, in addition to unemployment relief, the employment policies of advanced nations also include reinforcement of employability, apprentice systems, group consultation, technical licensing, and community work to supplement the main system.

Volunteer participation among private departments can also have a major impact on social security systems based largely on social welfare. This is because many measures for the care and support of the needy are designed with an eye toward getting the individual back into society as a productive member of the workforce, explaining why social security expenses are regarded as a kind of social investment. If these support measures benefit from the direct participation of regular citizens, rather than spending money on experts, it can go far in strengthening a sense of reciprocity throughout society at large. Increased sensitivity toward individual causality and reduction of hostility and anti-social conduct throughout society are synergistic factors, as well as key means for enhancing social security.

Humanity's ideals cannot ignore environmental reality. For those disadvantaged in global competition, **the state must provide social welfare with a social investment orientation,** to enable adjustment to global competition or involvement in localized production structure to achieve the aims of social security. That said, it cannot be independent from the operation and existence of the economic market, as they are often intertwined —sometimes mutually beneficial and at others mutually antagonistic.

With the age of global capitalism upon us, multinational capital flows where cost is lowest, and the exodus of investment means increased unemployment, exerting a tremendous impact on the people's lives and warning the people that the ideal of social welfare cannot be taken too far.

Welfare and economics appear antagonistic at first, yet they are actually part and parcel of one another. If we pay equal attention to welfare and economics at the same time, welfare should play the role of not worsening the investment environment, while at the same time serving as a structural security valve against unemployment — a difficult task indeed. Therefore, confronting socio-economic issues in the future, economists and welfare experts must not push each other around and assign blame on one another, but should establish common objectives and cooperate to achieve them together.

As I proposed earlier: **Establishing a three-way partnership between government, business, and private departments** to forge opportunities for all and prevent ineffectiveness and waste of public resources, should be the focus of efforts as Taiwan works to expand social security.

Many Taiwanese understand little about welfare systems, mistakenly believing that social welfare means people can get something for nothing, when in fact this is not what it's about. **Modern social welfare depends on the power of different groups to support**

Chapter Nine

one another. **Every individual should contribute during his or her productive years, and most countries have set conditions for minimal contribution to the system.** I do not idealistically believe that, when it comes to the design of the social welfare system, it is unnecessary to consider the selfish and greedy side of human nature; on the contrary, **only a thorough, equitable system will not "entice" people to violate the spirit of the system.** As we work towards achieving the objectives of social security, we must take special care in this area.

Even more so, I hope that in the future, by gradually building a "green silicon island," we can eliminate from the new social structure the agonizing tensions pervading today's society, and begin to move in the direction of the ideal world described in Sun Yatsen's essay *On the Practice of Civility.*

Chapter Ten

Towards a Green Silicon Island Distinguished by Mutual Trust

Confronted with the future challenges of global change, 21st century Taiwan must forge the room to triumph. With the vision for a Green Silicon Island as our blueprint, Taiwan will enhance competitiveness through nationwide learning and study, eliminate internal tensions, and progressively build from partnership towards a society of mutual trust. I have put this vision in the form of a letter to Taiwan's youth of the future.

Green Silicon Island —Taiwan's future in the face of global change

Before the existence of mankind, the energy cycle including the sun, land, air, and water formed our ecosystem. This system continues to deeply affect human activity, as well as the cycles governing materials and life such as minerals, animals, and plants. The energy, material, and living resources transmitted along the natural environment's pathways have always been the most basic foundation for human survival on this planet.

During the preliminary stage of human civilization, humans relied on conquering nature to reap resources and ensure security for survival. By the rise of industrial civilization, in addition to heavy mining of natural resources, people turned even further toward exploitation of labor for profit. And while industrialized technology raised the level of human living, supporting a larger population, it exacted the cost of widespread environmental destruction and the rapid reduction, even extinction, of natural species.

Looking back over the development of industrial civilization, initial development brought improved living conditions for humanity; however, grave environmental pollution and destruction have begun to turn against us, threatening the environment of human existence. Such side effects as the "greenhouse effect," the destruction of the ozone layer, and pollution of air and water resources were never anticipated by the architects of industrial technology.

The above factors underscore the need for mankind to pause for self-reflection. We must become more humble, more alert, contemplate the meaning of our existence and the value of life, and forge the future of human life on this planet.

Four centuries ago, Taiwan's aborigines had already inhabited this island for tens of thousands of years. Confronting the tests of nature, they had long developed a culture of symbiotic co-existence with the land. Four centuries ago, the arrival of the Dutch, who built Fort Zeelandia in the town of Anping as the stronghold of the Dutch East India Company, established Taiwan's initial connections with Western civilization. Again, as was her fickle fate, Taiwan under Japanese colonial rule took her first steps toward industrialization.

Following World War Two, in line with the formation of the Cold War order, with the help of American aid the Kuomintang regime developed processing export zones, driving the robust economic growth of the 1960s and 70s. Tasting the fruits of industrial civilization for the first time, Taiwan leapt into position as one of Asia's "Four Little Dragons."

Faced with the historical changes over the past four centuries in Taiwan, our thinking must take a step down, becoming more humble, like the ripe rice shoots of the Chianan Plains —the fuller they become the lower their tips bow down towards the ground. Given the limited nature of the resources at our disposal, integration of resources demands extensive consideration and investigation. Nevertheless, the challenges mounting before us, like the onset of a summer typhoon, do not allow us a moment's hesitation. Faced with such global phenomena as shifts in the global climate, changes in the industry structure, the acceleration of capital flow, and innovation in technology and information, our determination to meet these challenges must be stronger than ever.

As a political conduit, a responsible politician must consider how to adjust viable political conduct on all fronts to promote Taiwan's local adjustment policy. **I believe that adopting cooperation in place of opposition, and mutual benefit instead of exploitation to establish new partnerships between people and people, and between people and nature, is critical for human society of the future.**

The establishment of new partnerships must begin with reconciliation between humanity and nature, with the understanding that man's dominion over nature is not a given, but demands necessary self-restraint. Such a humble civilized attitude towards nature is the key to assimilating the man-made environment into the natural environment. This way, human activities will become a part of the natural environment, and by the same token the natural environment becomes a part of the man-made environment. This is especially vital when we realize that conventional economic growth exacted at the cost of material depletion has come to the end of the line, and that retrenchment of natural resource consumption is an inevitable trend. Still, in another sense, **the move away from materialism toward spiritual consumption and virtual simulation is just beginning to take form. Moreover, its scope will extend far beyond that of the original material economy. Hence, rather than standing at the edge of the pond longing for fish, we should set about making a net,**

taking practical steps to prepare for the changes ahead.

Taiwan is especially lacking in natural resources. Our past achievements have all been built upon a large supply of inexpensive white and blue collar labor, while turning to complete reliance on the use of raw materials and energy from abroad. In light of this situation, our resource problem is more urgent than that of most others, but we are fortunate to have equally first-rate information technology. Taiwan's high tech industry, concentrated in Hsinchu City and environs, has become a world-class OEM manufacturing base for computer hardware, while software development has also begun to demonstrate world-class capacity. This is why this trend is both a crisis and a potential turn for the better. To ensure the latter, we must respond quicker than other nations.

Envisioning the future of human living, I have long dreamed of a Green Valley. I imagine people in the future sharing the beauty of nature and the convenience of high tach at the same time. I cannot conceive of where the two are incompatible. On the other hand, I have long considered the coexistence of high industrialization and environmental destruction today to be a mistake of human history, and am optimistic that changes can be made to offset this mistake. I think this time has nearly arrived, and that Taiwan can lead the way, achieving this dream a step ahead of others.

In line with Taiwan's current conditions, moving toward this idea, expanding the blueprint to cover the entire island of Taiwan, and employing the existing high tech industry in the service of the future Taiwan, we can coin a new description of Taiwan: the Green Silicon

Island. I hope that this can become another name for Taiwan within this millennium.

First, we must complete the establishment of a green infrastructure throughout the island, forming a new consumption structure based on spiritual and cultural consumption, as opposed to material retrenchment and energy consumption, leveraging the stress of change into a new occasion for transformation. We should make national land planning into the center of green living, recycling materials in livable space to minimize energy dissipation. At the same time, we should accelerate the development of biochemical science based on agricultural technology to **forge a symbiotic partnership between man and the living realm in which mankind is a participant in the symbiotic cycle.** We should minimize the scope of urban areas, reducing commute time and energy costs, gradually separating into widely dispersed settlements, so that small towns become the basic functional unit of life. Using transportation and communication links, we can connect everyone together into a networked community, completing Green Silicon Island's hardware structure.

Next —and even more importantly —using the momentum of humanity's shift towards spiritual consumption demand, and employing the software and hardware tools at our disposal in information-related industries, we must collaborate with technologically advanced countries to develop and accelerate development of virtual reality research, and evolve related commodities. This way, we can guide the overall Taiwanese economy towards an information economy and intellectual economy based on spiritual consumption and virtual consumption. At the same time, we allow the transfer of already inappropriate conventional industries to China, to develop China's coastal region into an economic sphere inextricably linked to Taiwan's interests, forming a buffer zone for Taiwanese industry. In sum, shifting material consumption industries offshore and introducing spiritual consumption industries to Taiwan and accelerating their development, we bring about the grand transformation of Taiwan's industry structure.

Preparing for the arrival of an era based on spiritual consumption and supplemented by material consumption, cultural and educational policies must be retooled to make cultural preservation and transmission of civilization our top priority. Given Taiwan's position in the Oriental cultural sphere, it is incumbent upon Taiwan to establish a spiritual benchmark for Oriental civilization. As opposed to analytical Western thinking, Taiwan should develop a model of inclusive thinking, embracing Western civilization within that model, to realize the fusion of a trans-cultural vision within the spiritual realm. Having achieved such a high degree of spiritual achievement, in the new era of spiritual and virtual consumption, Taiwan will be able to establish the strategic high ground.

In the era of virtual consumption, electronic transactions and Internet commerce takes place across a global network of inter-connected computers and satellites with the byte as the basic unit of information transfer. With virtual contact among people enables informational exchange on an unprecedented scale, spiritual civilization and ideology face radical transformation. Taiwan will have the opportunity to take part in China's modernization, so that China enters a developed state faster. Winning friendship with amity, and eliminating the risks of conflict, a new window for cross-strait peace can unfold. Whether such a win-win situation is achieved depends entirely on our success in implementing the program for building Taiwan into a Green Silicon Island.

Standing at this time and place, Taiwan is bursting with possibility. Yet we must raise our expectations of ourselves, and stride boldly forward.

From partnership towards a "trust" society

Yesterday's victors won't necessarily pass today's tests, and tomorrow is an unknown black box: We can make wishes or draw up plans, but we can never be completely sure, for the world is always changing and will continue to keep changing. At the dawn of the 21st century, Taiwan —like any people, nation or regional organization in the world —faces an unknown situation, yet an unknown situation shared globally. Here, the big boys are not guaranteed unobstructed passage, while the little boys, to a similar degree, enjoy less limited options. Not to mention, given the ebb and flow dynamics between the large and small, the outcome depends on how one chooses objectives and works toward their achievement.

Cold Realpolitik calculations remain one of the basic issues that we must handle cautiously. Still, in addition to these complex considerations, we must balance development between mechanisms of "calculation of interests" and "mutual trust," eliminating friction at home and in the international arena at the root to forge a more open realm. This way, Taiwan —our foothold on the world —will have greater opportunities for contact, dialogue, and cooperation on a global scale, ensuring our hard-earned voice and right to survival. Consequently, Taiwan should establish partnerships with nations around the world in line with the ebb and flow of state power, and contribute as a participant in global risk management policy to elevate Taiwan's substantive condition and status.

Each individual, each group, and each nation is qualified to claim its interests from its own position. Still, every self-serving position can potentially trigger an even stronger self-serving stance, deliberate or not. When self-serving perspectives are strengthened, each ego (self) only becomes more closed and harder to understand. Shut out, the individual wonders why the world in which he exists is so cold, disordered, and inaccessible.

How does one escape the bottleneck of self-service? Simply, it only takes loosening up the hard line of individuals, groups, or nations who insist that "it must be this way" or "I have no choice" when it comes to numerous issues, and providing the possibility of other options. This gives others a chance to take part in the risk game of "it appears good, and looks harmless on the surface," fostering trust out of limited cooperative experience in the attempt to achieve partnership.

Wherever there is "trust" there is "risk"; however, this is the most basic means of expressing or hoping for goodwill, and in contrast to

The Son of Taiwan

free choice it allows both sides the space to continue, wait and see, or exit at any time in the process of "trying / making mistakes."

This is also why I am in favor of establishing partnerships between various levels within Taiwan's government, so that local governments can truly become local governments —the hubs of local consumption and living —the provider of infrastructure construction, the center of regional development, and the promoter of local adaptation to globalization. Within our own society, we must establish partnerships between the government and the private sector, working gradually from experience and transforming that experience into relationships of trust in society, paving a firm cultural foundation for the mature civil society of Taiwan's future.

Undeniably, the Kuomintang's unchanging attitude toward the regime's longstanding authoritarian rule has induced constant threats from hegemonic China, hindering the development of mutual trust among the Taiwanese, whether on the domestic on international political front. Meanwhile, political and commercial factions and the "material exchanges" between organized crime and government officials are predicated on shared interests and supplemented by "face." These popular relationships of trust constantly skirt the outer perimeter of the law, unable to expand beyond the scope of "our kind of people." We must have the courage to reform this highly corrosive, murky bond of trust, cracking open all units and incidents maligned by the people in an open, transparent, convenient fashion. Meanwhile, we shall constantly loosen the grip of self-interested, contemptuous means of expression domestically and internationally, to implement trust at the level of the people's daily lives **so that "risks worth taking are equal** to trust" becomes part of the popular consciousness. This way, we will possess the power to handle the increasingly elusive challenges of the 21st century.

You trust Taiwan, Taiwan trusts you.

This shall be our pact.

Escaping the shadow of ethnic problems

Taiwan is an immigrant society. For thousands of years, beginning with aborigines, people came to Taiwan from many different countries and races. Some came and went, and others had families and settled down. This is why, when I think about ethnic and cultural issues, I always want to extend the depth of history, approaching history from the standpoint of the land rather than from the perspective of humans.

That said, separating the issues of "people" and "the land" is often more difficult than it seems. For instance, what should be done when contradictions of interests emerge among different ethnic groups? When members of different ethnic groups have different views toward the land, then what do we do? I believe that as a "home-grown" political party born in Taiwan and loyal to the land, the Democratic Progressive party is not only responsible for mitigating these tensions, but we are also obligated to declare that **the DPP is a party for**

everyone, and not just a single ethnic group. Indeed, the DPP should work to secure the highest interests of all Taiwanese.

Growing up in the countryside of Tainan County, the village was almost entirely populated by Hoklo people, with no Hakkas, no mainlanders, and even less chance of aborigines settling there. It was only when I came to Taipei for university that I had many more opportunities to get to know and make friends with people from other ethnic groups. Once, a classmate from a family of mainlanders invited me to his home for dinner. His father, a veteran who had come to Taiwan with the Kuomintang, regaled me with stories of the war against Japan, making a distinct impression on me.

Involvement in politics has afforded me still greater opportunities to exchange views with others, and to appreciate the different stories and circumstances of our various ethnic groups. I know that there are worthwhile cultural aspects in every group, and that we should offer caring and support to the disadvantaged in society. However, in recent years, it has become fashionable to equate discussion of ethnic issues with "stirring up ethnic tensions." I strongly disagree with this notion. Claiming that Taiwan has no ethnic issues cannot resolve the disadvantaged status of aborigines over time, nor can it prevent repeated instances of voting for one's second choice just to keep a member of another ethnic group from getting elected —a harmful side effect of Taiwanese democracy. Rather, only by facing ethnic issues squarely and coolly contemplating Taiwan's interests can we forge a new Taiwanese family distinguished by equal rights and mutual trust.

In the future, no matter which party controls the levers of state power, ethnic-blind, talent-exclusive policy will be indispensable. I must underscore that "disregard of race" is a canon of democracy, and "ethnic balancing" is a myth. Concerning aborigine policy, in taking into account the unique lifestyle and cultural background of aborigines, **we must respect the natural sovereignty of aborigines, and widen their autonomy with an eye toward the ultimate goal of turning over aborigine matters to aborigines.**

All cultures, Hoklo, Hakka, aboriginal, the culture transplanted with *Waishengren* to Taiwan, or even the lifestyles of the foreign laborers who have recently arrived in Taiwan, have a unique historical progression and flow, a distinctive traditional wisdom, and in the long historical progression of humanity on earth, an indelible position. Even if seen from a narrow local perspective, each of these elements enriches Taiwanese culture, giving the land more fertile seeds. For our part, the efforts we make for culture help preserve the diversity of the human gene pool. For only by preserving different genes can the human race adapt to the unpredictable changes of the future and continue to evolve.

It is comforting to note that despite a history of sadness and subjugation over the past centuries, a young "new national consciousness" has gradually taken shape over the recent period of democratization. Here's hoping that, armed with this consciousness, Taiwan can say goodbye to sadness and set upon autonomous development.

This "new national consciousness" is our response to the goodness of the land that has nurtured us, as well as a product of history we must appreciate and treasure.

Nevertheless, as this "new national consciousness" takes shape, we must never lose sight of the idea that while each of us is a passer-by on this land in the greater scheme of history, during our lifetimes we are the land's masters. Every person living on the land is qualified to express his views on Taiwan's future, because Taiwan's future is our future.

Educational policy: the central role of learning

Taiwan's capacity to compete in the 21st century shall be determined by the quality of her human resources or manpower. So where education is concerned, all I have to say is: educational reform must continue.

Over the past decade, thanks to the efforts of Dr. Lee Yuan-tseh and educational reformers in the private sector, educational reform has taken its first agonizing steps. Still, we must look ahead to the future for tangible results. The saying "it takes ten years to grow trees, but a hundred to rear people" is not only apropos regarding education, but similarly germane to educational reform.

When I was in school, getting in to the next level of schooling was the most important thing. Testing into a good school was the only means to casting off the burden of family poverty, thus poor families wanted nothing more than for their children to possess good character and the ability to perform well in school. Today, however, this concept is clearly a bit outdated, as a degree is no longer a safeguard and examples abound of successful people who never even obtained a university degree. Clearly, the time has come to readjust the objectives of education in Taiwan.

After years of promotion by private sector education reformers, **I believe that "people-based" education remains an appropriate goal and utmost ideal.** Elementary and middle school students should be able to develop their minds and bodies in school, learning how to get along with others and getting to know their own abilities.

Today, elementary and middle schools have strengthened local awareness and native language education, but strengthening the relationships between schools and communities —**to let students feel that they are not just part of a family but also a greater community** —is even more important. This signifies that primary and middle school educational programs should be more "localized." Government units at the city, county, town, and village levels must not just take their due educational rights from the central government, but must take responsibility for the quality of elementary and primary school education.

We must look to see if pre-school educational opportunities are fair, and how to promote the acceptance of problem students and drop-outs into the community, for education is the upstream realm of public safety.

In the area of higher education, we must think in a different direction. Faced with a future world of global competition, students must possess excellent competitiveness necessary to adjust to this competitive world. At the same time, **top caliber higher educational manpower is the lifeblood of Taiwan's continued development.** With this in mind, we must enhance the research capacity of focus universities. This means pouring more resources into certain individual universities, not simply allocating equal funding to each institution, for this is an essential tactic for establishing Taiwan's preeminence in select academic disciplines, and achieving the objective of keeping talent in Taiwan and even attracting outstanding talents to work and live in Taiwan.

Perhaps compared to the world's prestigious institutions, Taiwan's universities are too young and somewhat limited in certain respects, yet by the same token they carry no excess baggage and possess tremendous flexibility, equipping us to mesh well with new technology. For example, the Massachusetts Institute of Technology (MIT), Harvard University's neighbor, has gained tremendous prestige with its Media Lab, representing a vital marriage with the information industry. MIT's approach is an ideal example for Taiwan, as we make the shift toward the intellectual economy. Bangkok University, focusing on Asian developmental experience as its main research field, is also an excellent model for Taiwanese business schools.

Naturally, I am aware that not everybody can become involved in global competitive industries, and that a certain proportion of the population will remain in local industries, working hard to build a better local living environment. Once education has been freed up, research-oriented higher education must change, taking a selecting approach to knowledge so as to distill its finest essence. Further, we must create new interfaces between general practitioners and specialists, and between users of knowledge and research specialists. In so doing, promoting mutually beneficial cooperation, we can stride toward an intellectual economy and e-commerce based on "full knowledge work." This is the foremost task for higher education in the future.

In addition, we must provide more opportunities for vocational education, the objectives of which include hands-on experience over formulaic theory. Given the rapid rate of change in the know-how required to keep up with the demands of work, lifetime education must be made as convenient and diverse as possible so that anyone who needs to learn can continue to enjoy extensive learning resources beyond the conclusion of their formal education.

In order to achieve these objectives, the realignment of the educational system is unavoidable. I understand that the greatest impediment to educational reform in recent years has not been the students or the parents, but has come from the people who hold educational resources in their hands. Yet without the full participation of principals and teachers, the process of educational reform becomes exponentially more difficult. In the future, I hope that by doing away with inessential testing systems we can enhance the substance and esteem of teaching work, making education an interesting, creative occupation. I am sure our students will benefit greatly from such change.

Education is an undertaking of the "mind." Only by setting our minds on considering the objectives of education, energizing the substance and methods of education, and upgrading the quality of education on all fronts, can we cultivate the next generation with the skills needed to face an unknown world.

An open letter to Young Taiwan

Dear Chih-chung:

Remember that day I saw you chatting with a cyber friend? You said he lives in Canada, and like you he is studying law, giving you a lot to talk about. Standing behind you, I was strongly impressed that a completely new world has already appeared behind my back. And when I turn around to see it, it feels both alluring and unfamiliar.

Your sister and mother are closer, and you and I have more in common. Today, I want to write you a sincere letter.

In the new Information Age, "customized news" and "personal TV" are right at your fingertips. Compared to our generation, which bled and sweated in the fight for freedom of speech and information, yours is a totally different experience. Thanks to your fondness for American movies, you know more colloquial English than (my native language of) Hoklo Taiwanese. Over the Internet, Canada, far away in North America, is perhaps closer to you than your grandmother's home in the Tainan countryside.

I'm happy to see all these changes. Because on the Internet, there is greater parity in relationships among people, completely usurping the authoritarianism remnant in our society. Moreover, for Taiwanese living on an island, the Internet affords us an additional interface for contact with the world, opening up avenues for direct dialogue with the world. Our society was once extremely authoritarian, once particularly closed, but thanks to the sacrifice and dedication of generation upon generation, our society has broken free of that past. I'm so pleased that your generation need not carry those burdens and that you can enjoy wide open possibilities.

I look at members of Taiwan's new generation as they come to me to sign their "A-Bian Family" hats, and I feel as though I'm seeing you. I think that in addition to your passion for abundant information, diverse human relations and video games, a feeling of powerlessness toward society overwhelms your generation. Otherwise, you wouldn't always wear such a cynical expression on your face when you read the paper, you wouldn't feel confounded by your future at times, or knit your brow in anger at the things around you. I am familiar with all these situations from my youth, and only the means of expression have really changed.

Young people have the privilege to be disappointed with society. Please remember, you always have the right to feel disappointed by society, whether or not your father is a political figure. Even if your father is fortunate enough to serve as the nation's leader, you can be displeased with me and point out my mistakes all the same. Your generation of youths has the responsibility to use your own ways to raise your own issues and continue to improve this society. You are the future, so of course you must go out and make your mark on the world.

A sociologist has noted that in order to effect societal change when communications are restricted, change must come in the form of breakthroughs, the way the Kaohsiung Incident lit the torch of democracy for Taiwan. However, in an era of free communications, minute change is constantly taking place so that each issue appears inconsequential. Does this mean that the younger generation is powerless to engender societal change on a greater scale? Of course not. But it must be produced in your own way.

Perhaps we belong to different generations, but please remember that the succession of changes brought about by outside forces in Taiwan over the past 400 years, no matter what kind of forces were involved, have all had a decisive impact on Taiwanese history. In the future, this trend will not only continue, it will only gain intensity. In a rapidly changing world, intellectual changes are equally rapid, so you must maintain the capacity to learn throughout your life in order to handle the requirements for knowledge your life demands.

Never forget this: Taiwan has a different historical clock from that of other countries in the world. Although global information pathways enable us to receive information quicker than ever, in synch with the rest of the world, **our thinking must remain rooted in Taiwan, taking into consideration such aspects as our concern for the land and the depth of Taiwanese history.** This way, we can meet the world with a distinctive approach. Similarly, we can apply all that we learn to our environment in Taiwan.

In the future, apart from bundled intellectual theory, hands-on knowledge is especially important. Speaking one's mind about something is a good thing, but by taking action and doing something you can learn a great deal more. Just like I see you with computers and video games, often you just get right into the action, learning naturally without having to consult an instruction booklet. The world works the same way —you mustn't lock yourself inside. Get out, make friends, relate to people, and try everything you're interested in, and you'll learn quicker and even more.

Especially now that the new millennium is upon us, Western nations with Judeo-Christian heritage will consider the events of history, and looking towards the work ahead, will propose numerous plans for the future. Taiwan, as a member of Asian civilization, should also learn from this spirit, greeting the new century with new leadership and a new blueprint for the future. As a member of Taiwan's young generation, you must put your creative spirit to work to forge a future that belongs to you and to all of Taiwan. My generation will age steadily, gradually exiting the stage. Nothing can stop the trends of history, and just like Taiwan's previous shift from the agricultural era towards the industrial era, now we are entering the Information Age. This future belongs to your generation of young Taiwanese.

In order that Taiwan has a more competitive future, our generation will give our best efforts today, and defer to you and your generation. When that time comes, and it will come sooner than later, I hope you will have done everything necessary to take charge.

Bless you in your life!
Dad

The Son of Taiwan
——The Life of Chen Shui-Bian and his dreams for Taiwan

Copyright © 2000,Taiwan Publishing Co.Ltd.
P.O.Box1418, Upland, CA 91785 U.S.A.
Tel:909-985-9458   Fax:909-985-5600

望春風文化事業股份有限公司
台灣104台北市中原街 3 號
3, Chungyuan St. Taipei, Taiwan
Tel:886-2-2563-4650   Fax:886-2-2563-8448

Printed in Taiwan

ISBN 957-97979-4-3（平裝）

US$ 20